KATHY COLLARD MILLER

Partly Cloudy
with
Scattered
Worries

BETHANYHOUSE
PUBLISHERS
MINNEAPOLIS, MINNESOTA

Published by Bethany House Publishers
11400 Hampshire Avenue South
Bloomington, Minnesota 55438

Bethany House Publishers is a division of
Baker Publishing Group, Grand Rapids, Michigan.

Printed in the United States of America

Library of Congress Cataloging-in-Publication Data

Miller, Kathy C. (Kathy Collard)
  Partly cloudy with scattered worries : finding peace in all kinds of weather / by Kathy Collard Miller.
  p. cm.
  Summary: "Explores why women tend to worry and offers imaginative and time-proven steps to help gain victory over anxiety. Topics include fear of the future, how love casts out fear, how prayer alleviates worry, how to overcome anxiety, and more. Conversational, practical, filled with stories, biblically based, with discussion questions"—Provided by publisher.
  Includes bibliographical references.
  ISBN 0-7642-0025-9 (pbk.)
  1. Christian women—Religious life. 2. Worry—Religious aspects—Christianity. 3. Peace of mind—Religious aspects—Christianity. I. Title.
  BV4527.M445   2005
  248.8'43—dc22

                                                    2004024664

Partly Cloudy
with
Scattered
Worries

DEDICATION

Donald Miller, my father-in-law,
who was willing to have his heart changed by God.

JANUARY 19, 1914–FEBRUARY 3, 2004

CONTENTS

PROLOGUE 11
Dense Fog Predicted
Is it Fear, Careful Thought, or Worry?

CHAPTER 1 15
Anticipating a Storm
What You Fear May Be the Greatest Blessing
So Many Reasons to Fret . . . Our First Solution . . . Going Deeper . . . The "Good" of Cancer . . . Jochebed

CHAPTER 2 29
Walking on the Sunny Side
Perfect Love Casts Out Fear
God Is Pure Love . . . God Is Perfect Love . . . God Is Prudent Love . . . Rebekah

CHAPTER 3 45
Catching the Rainbow
How Prayer Alleviates Worry
Pray! . . . Stay! . . . Obey! . . . Hannah

CHAPTER 4 61
Don't Forget Your Umbrella
How Gratitude Protects Your Heart
Appreciation . . . Attention . . . Acclamation . . . Michal

CHAPTER 5 77
Seeing Past the Snowstorm
How God's Sovereignty Provides
It's All About God, Not About You! . . . It's All About Him, Not About You . . . But You Are Important! . . . It's All About God; It's Not About Your Stature! . . . It's All About God; It's Not About Clothing! . . . It's All About God, Not About Tomorrow! . . . Naomi

CHAPTER 6 93

April Showers Bring May Flowers

Seeing the Purpose in Troubles

Don't Be Surprised! . . . Do Be Steadfast! . . . Don't Resist Stretching . . . Abigail

CHAPTER 7 109

Ice Storm

How to Keep Worry From Slipping Into Controlling Others

Worry Can't Communicate Love . . . Worry Can't Change Others . . . Worry Can't Control Others . . . Salome

CHAPTER 8 125

Rain Behind You

How the Past Can Cloud the Present

Remember, But Don't Regret . . . Remember, But Forgive . . . Remember, But Look Forward . . . Miriam

CHAPTER 9 139

Tornado a-Comin'

Finding the Storm Cellar of God's Power

God Can Do Whatever He Wants, He's Experienced . . . God Can Do All He Wants, He's Extravagant . . . God Can Do However He Wants, He's Exacting . . . God Can Do Whenever He Wants, He's Expeditious . . . Esther

EPILOGUE 157

Windy Day

Having the Spirit Flow in Your Life

SUGGESTIONS FOR GROUP LEADERS 161

ENDNOTES 165

ABOUT THE AUTHOR 169

ACKNOWLEDGMENTS

$\mathcal{I}$'m grateful for the input and insights that so many have given me. Thank you to Leslie Collard, Karen Dellosso, Gayle DeSalles, Karen Dye, Robbie Estridge, Melanie Hubbard, Estella Olin, Darlene Rusnak, Christi Anne Sheppeard, and Ginny Yttrup.

You'll read the stories of many different people in this book. I'm very grateful to the men and women who shared their hearts, struggles, and victories.

I'm so grateful for my agent, Janet Kobobel Grant, for her wisdom, guidance, and patience. Thank you also to my editors, Julie Smith and Jeanne Hedrick, who edited with sensitivity and discernment.

As always, I want to acknowledge my husband, Larry, who is the love of my life, my encourager and supporter, and who out-serves me through his helpfulness and open heart. Thank you, my love, for all that you mean to me.

I'm totally in awe of my Lord God and Master Jesus, who gives me one assignment after another. Father, I want you to be made larger and more personal in the eyes of others. Thank you for the privilege of representing you to others.

PROLOGUE

Dense Fog Predicted

Is it Fear, Careful Thought, or Worry?

*I'*ll never forget that Christmas Eve in the Los Angeles basin. I was eight years old, and we had gone to my grandparents' home for our celebration. But when we left their home around nine o'clock that evening, a dense fog had socked in the area—so thick that we couldn't see within ten feet of the house. We climbed into the car and headed down familiar streets for the thirteen miles to our home . . . slowly. Very slowly. My mother got behind the wheel and my father walked directly in front of the car trying to see ahead. At times he literally disappeared into the fog, and my heart leapt in my throat. I was terrified! And what made it worse was that we heard voices of people who were crying out, in seeming pain.

"Mom!" I said, my voice rising in nervousness. "Those people need help! Do you hear them?"

"Yes, Kathy, I do," my mom replied. "But it's just kids playing a joke. It's really okay, sweetie."

I tried to calm my palpitating heart, but I just sat in the backseat, worried! We made it home safely that night, but I've never forgotten that experience.

Sometimes when I'm worried, I feel like a fog of fear and anxiety is swirling all around me, blocking out the ability to think clearly and trust God. It quickly fuels responses like complaining, grumbling, or making a quick decision that isn't led by God.

As I begin to worry, I remember that I'm a Christian and I'm not supposed to worry. So my defense mechanisms kick in. I reason:

I'm not worried, I'm just *thinking*!

I'm not worried, I'm just *wondering*!

I'm not worried, I'm just *concerned*!

I'm not worried, I'm just *mulling over a problem*!

I'm not worried, I'm just *a little bothered*!

But then honesty rears its unwelcome head, and I surrender. Okay! I'm *worried*!

I've gone through this scenario many times. It's so easy to deceive myself into thinking I'm not worried—I'm just thinking too much. Besides, don't I need to plan just in case something terrible happens? But at a certain point, thinking, wondering, being concerned, mulling, or being bothered becomes worry. And at that point, I'm not trusting God with my whole heart.

Fear, Careful Thought, or Worry?

Now, there is indeed a difference between fear, careful thought, and worry. *Fear* can be a legitimate emotion, serving as God's warning signal to do something—QUICK! (As in, that bear coming toward you looks really hungry!) Fear can turn into worry, though, if we (1) don't take action (like scream or play dead!); or (2) we fail to release control because we recognize that we have no power over the situation or person (doesn't apply to the bear analogy—we can do something).

Fear in itself is not sinful when it's based on something truly dangerous. If your daughter is late getting home from a date, you might feel fearful for a legitimate reason. But it doesn't have to turn to worry if you do something constructive—like pray for her safety.

Careful thought is what our mind does when faced with an uncertain situation or problem. That's to be expected. God wants us to use the mind He's given us.

But as we try to figure out the solution, our careful reasoning can easily slide into worry if we don't turn our attention to God, to ask for His input and trust Him. If your daughter is late getting home from that date, careful thought is necessary; you might take the action of calling her cell phone.

When the Bible talks about worry, it's not referring to fear or careful thought. *Worry* is not the same as insightful planning or feeling responsible for something that is legitimately our responsibility. Worry is when our thoughts are wrapped in a haze of anxiety that discounts God's ability to help us. *Merriam-Webster Dictionary* (online) says that, at its source, the word *worry* carries the idea of choking or strangling, along with torment. We begin to worry because we don't turn to God or, if we do, we don't release the fear to Him. If your daughter is late getting home from that date, you might pace the floor and imagine her already dead in an auto accident. And when she walks in the door, your worry may turn into an urge to kill—that's when worry is choking us and controlling our actions!

How much is worry strangling us? Anxiety is currently the number one emotional problem of American people. Panic anxiety is the number one mental-health problem for women in the United States, and in men it's second only to substance abuse.[1] Dr. Archibald Hart states that one research group at Pennsylvania State University defined worry as "a chain of negative and relatively uncontrollable thoughts and images." He also states that about 15 percent of the population can be classified as chronic worriers. That's about one person out of seven. A chronic worrier is defined as someone who worries more than an hour and a half a day.[2] Most of us would sigh with relief and say, "Oh, thank goodness! I guess I don't worry too much, because I don't worry *that* much."

But I've noticed that a lot of my worry is something I don't readily recognize. I prefer to call it *concerned, mulling,* or *thinking.* But when I'm honest with myself, I recognize that I actually am worried, because my thoughts are not centered in trust in God. I'm trying to figure out the situation myself. Even if I can't take action, I continue to think it over, like a cow chewing its cud. (But it sure isn't nourishing!)

At a speaking engagement I asked the women in the audience, "At what point does mulling or thinking about a problem become worry?" I was surprised when the women gave answers like "ten minutes" or "fifteen minutes." One woman said, "five minutes."

Ouch! I'm guilty! How about you? Just in the last several days I've noticed my thinking spilling over onto the side of worry. Two couples are coming to stay for the weekend. One couple we know, the other is friends of the couple. *How will we spend our time? Are they nice? Will we get along?* All these questions swirl in my mind and, before I know it, I'm wringing my hands, convinced we won't have a good time.

Or I begin thinking, *I can't believe I said that to her—that was so insensitive! I just know she's not going to want to be my friend anymore.*

Your worries may include concern about work, singleness, children, a husband involved in pornography, or a million other things. How can we cope with active minds, wondering what the future holds?

If you're relating to these feelings, then I invite you to journey with me through this book. I'm eager to join you as we delve into how we can diminish worry. It *is* possible! Whether you are a chronic worrier or someone just looking for greater peace from occasional worry, you'll find in this book the keys to peace and contentment, which are held in believing and feeling the truths of

- God's love, sovereignty, and power;
- the effectiveness of prayer;
- the protection of gratitude;
- seeing the purpose in our fears;
- not trying to control others; and
- releasing past regrets.

We'll also peek into the lives of biblical women like Jochebed, Rebekah, Hannah, Michal, and others to see what they can teach us about resisting worry and trusting God instead. As you read about these women in the Bible you won't find the word *worry* connected with them. For instance, Scripture doesn't say, "And Hannah was worried that she'd never get pregnant." But there is no doubt that the challenges they faced could, and probably did, create worry for them. I know that I would have worried in all of their situations! So let's probe a little deeper than the events recorded in Scripture and relate to how they must have felt about them. I know that won't be hard to do.

But wait! That's not all! You'll also receive (if you call within thirty minutes—oh, sorry, wrong commercial) discussion questions at the end of each chapter, along with a "Letter From God" that will enhance your study of the Bible by yourself or in a group.

Ready? I can't wait to see how God speaks to you. Let's go! The fog is about to lift!

CHAPTER 1

Anticipating a Storm

What You Fear May Be the Greatest Blessing

I headed out on my jog, eyeing the storm clouds that threatened rain above me. *Oh, I so want to run, and I can't run tomorrow. I've got to do it right now even if it rains.* But by the time I'd run a mile, the drops started and got bigger and bigger.

Oh! I'm so disappointed, I mourned, as I turned and headed back. But then, a new resolve overwhelmed me. *By golly, I'm going to run even if I get wet. It's just too important for my health.*

I continued running, and the drops fell continually but weren't drenching. As I ran the rain actually slackened, but clouds off in the distance were a dark, threatening color. *Will it hold off?* By the time I'd passed my three-mile mark the sprinkles had stopped, and when I looked up at the sky the dark clouds were gone. *Where did they go?* I turned to look for them, but they had dissipated. The sky was still overcast though.

For the next two miles no rain fell. As I reached the last half mile the storm clouds opened up again and my clothes were reaching the wet category. But I didn't care that my hair was wet. It had been an exhilarating run. Walking for my cooldown, I saw a few rays of sun break through the clouds, splashing the luscious, colorful hues of a rainbow across the sky. *Wow! I would have missed it if I hadn't risked getting wet.*

My run could have been a really unpleasant experience, but the warning of rain had turned out to be a worse threat than the actual rain. In the end, I was rewarded with a beautiful rainbow that I would have missed had I not run.

As I ran that day I saw an analogy to worry. Its growl is worse than its bite. Worry can easily cause us to focus on disaster while taking away our ability to trust God. Yet even if what we fear happens, it's often not as bad as we *thought* it would be. We might even experience the "rainbow" of God's blessings in some unexpected way.

So Many Reasons to Fret

But let's face it. It seems like there *is* a lot to worry about. Life's storms range from sprinkles to cloudbursts, even major tornados that can terrorize us. *Is my child being bullied at school? Will my husband lose his job, and can I keep mine? I'm single; will God provide that longed-for husband? Will I be carjacked?* A thousand and more reasons to fret, fume, and fear. Is it really possible to be at peace and trust God, especially when He doesn't always protect us from bad things?

Yes, it is possible, because God wants to give us peace. We were created to walk in fellowship with God, trusting Him for everything in our lives. We were *not* created with the capability of carrying a heavy load of worry. Many people think of worry as just an innocuous way to spend time, but it is actually destructive. When we take the wrong route, handling life with worry, our body reacts with ulcers, tension, and disease. As we'll discover in chapter 7, worry can also cause us to respond to the people around us with inappropriate reactions.

Yes, we do need to think, ponder, wonder, and consider . . . even think with care. But that is different than worry. Psalm 94:19 tells us, "When my anxious thoughts multiply within me, Your consolations delight my soul." Worry expands within the mind to crowd out trust in God. We begin to think we need to control and manipulate, to guarantee that nothing bad will happen. We feel tense, wondering if God can handle our situation. Even if we acknowledge that He can handle it, we wonder if He really cares and will respond to our need. When fear and distrust of His will for us crowds out trust, worry multiplies and creates destructive forces within us.

That's why God doesn't want us to worry. We were created for trust and rest and peace in Him. It's because God loves us and wants the best for us that He doesn't want us to worry. That's why worry is sin. Scripture commands us not to do it! If we do, we are being disobedient.

Like many other sins, we'll never overcome worry completely. But God does want us to learn to diminish it more and more, because it is a distraction to trusting Him. In the Bible the word *distraction* is most often translated "anxious" (NASB and NIV) and "careful" (Philippians 4:6 KJV: "Be careful for nothing").

Commentator Matthew Henry identifies that for us when he says about Philippians 4:6: "Here is a caution against disquieting perplexing care (v. 6): Be careful for nothing . . . avoid anxious care and distracting thought in the wants and difficulties of life."

Then he goes on to clarify, "It is the duty and interest of Christians to live without care. There is a care of diligence which is our duty, and consists in a wise forecast and due concern; but there is a care of diffidence and distrust which is our sin and folly, and which only perplexes and distracts the mind."[1]

Worry is sinful because it distracts us from calling upon God's solutions or intervention. Yet I am concerned (I didn't say worried!) that thinking of worry as sin will be discouraging to some. They might think, "Well, isn't that going a little too far? When I think of worry as sin, I feel condemned, since I can't seem to get rid of it completely."

No one can overcome it perfectly, but we can diminish its hold over us. When we recognize that we are worrying and that it is sinful, we can follow God's directions (1 John 1:9), which are applicable for any sin: Confess it, ask God for forgiveness, and receive His cleansing. That process is called repentance, and we'll need to go through those steps over and over again. But as we do we'll loosen the grip that worry has around our minds and hearts. And adding to that foundation, we will find many other truths and insights for finding and maintaining the peace that God wants us to enjoy. Let's look at our first insight.

Our First Solution

Although I can't stake any claim to conquering worry completely, many years ago, as a fairly new Christian, I heard a concept that began my mental and emotional transformation about worry. I attended Bill Gothard's "Basic Youth Conflicts" seminar, and he said, "Think of the worst possible thing that can happen and then think of reasons why it wouldn't be so bad after all," citing Romans 8:28, "And we know that God causes all things to work together for good to those who love God, to those who are called according to *His* purpose" (emphasis added).

Hmmm. *An interesting concept. Obviously scriptural.* I mulled it over, and then I got worried. *I don't think I want to give God the impression that He has my permission to do the worst possible thing!*

It seemed to be a risk, but my heart longed to be free from the nagging worries that ruled my life. I was nineteen or twenty, yet I felt like worry was my daily portion—like a storm cloud always threatening on the horizon. I had to *think about* how my friend may have misunderstood what I'd said. I had to *be concerned* about my grades in college. I had to *wonder* about my future. Of course, I used those innocuous words because I *worried* that someone would think I wasn't a strong Christian if I used the word *worry*. I felt tense, even condemned, because I knew God couldn't be pleased with me as a worrywart!

Then came the day I attended that seminar, and Bill's comment stood out in bold relief. *Can I apply it?* I decided I would try.

The day after the seminar I returned to my part-time job in the morning and college classes afterward. There were no extra minutes between the two. I often fretted about arriving late to class.

That morning I left work late because my boss pulled me aside to discuss something. As I drove, my stomach churned. I envisioned walking into the classroom late with all eyes on me and the teacher making some belittling comment. Then I remembered Bill Gothard's principle: "Think of the worst possible thing that can happen and then think of reasons why it wouldn't be so bad after all." I rehearsed Romans 8:28. *Here's my chance*, I mused. *What good thing could happen from being late?* I paused to try to think of something. *Okay . . . I'll be noticed. But that's the very thing I'm afraid of!*

I smiled. *But wait! I've been trying to share Christ with my fellow students. Maybe I can use being late to tell my new friend about how worried I was and how God gave me peace of mind.*

Bingo! With those thoughts, my anxiety level diminished. I couldn't wait to be late to class! I didn't need to drive like a maniac— God was going to use it!

Ten minutes later I walked into class without my typical breathlessness and was shocked to see that the teacher hadn't even arrived yet. *He* was late! I took my seat beside my new friend and I told her what happened. We laughed together.

That day I saw two truths about worry: God can bring good out of what we worry about, and most of the time what we worry about doesn't happen! The principle of Romans 8:28 began to diminish the hold that worry had over me.

About ten years after that college experience, I faced worry of another sort, and I didn't cope as well. At that time Larry and I had been married for seven years, and he was no longer my Prince Charming. In fact, I hated him! I felt unloved because he worked two jobs and flew airplanes for a hobby—rarely including me and our two children.

I was furious at him, and my anger created depression and abusive reactions toward our two-year-old daughter, Darcy. At times I kicked her, hit her in the head, and even choked her in my rages. I hated myself for hurting her, and even considered suicide as the only solution. I kept promising God I would never overreact again, and worried about the mental and emotional harm I was inflicting on Darcy.

One day as I stood near her I reached up to scratch my head. Darcy flinched as if she expected me to hit her. *O God! Darcy thinks I'm going to hurt her, without any provocation at all. How horrible! No, I'm horrible! She's terrified of me!*

My heart was broken. I worried, *She'll remember my anger forever; I just know it. There's no way she can ever grow up as a normal human being. And we'll never be friends when she's grown. She'll hate me forever. And Larry and I will most likely get a divorce, and then how can I ever claim to be a Christian?*

When I wasn't angry, fear and worry consumed my thoughts. I really believed I was capable of killing Darcy in one of my rages. I kept praying, "God, deliver me from my anger—I know you don't want me to be like this! Just take it away!"

When God didn't answer my prayer with an instantaneous deliverance, I worried that He no longer loved me or cared for me. *He's given up on me completely!* I fretted.

But what I didn't realize initially was that God wanted to answer my prayer in His own way—not through an instantaneous deliverance but through a process of growth that would bring freedom from my anger. Over a period of about a year God revealed the underlying causes of my anger and slowly gave me the solutions I needed. He taught me how to discipline Darcy without anger. He taught me that all anger is not wrong and that I can choose to control it. I also learned that I am a perfectionist, and I discovered how my perfectionistic tendencies created anger and frustration in me. In time, I asked for the emotional and prayer support of our women's neighborhood Bible study, and they held me accountable.

Little by little I became the loving, patient mother I really wanted to be, and Darcy responded with greater trust in me. She no longer cowered when I moved. And then God did the wonderful miracle of restoring the relationship between Larry and me. I couldn't believe it! It gave me peace of mind, but I still wondered what the long-range effects would be on our relationships.

God has been faithful and has brought good out of the bad. God created my ministry as I began to share through writing and speaking about God's work in my life. Through what I couldn't believe could be used for good—child abuse—God has brought abundant blessing: Thousands of women have been given hope in their own struggles. God is creative as He uses what we worry about to bring glory to His name. And now Larry and I speak and write together about marriage and how God healed our relationship. That's the truth of Romans 8:28.

But that doesn't mean we should plan on sinning or being careless about righteousness so that God can bring good from it. We shouldn't treat sin lightly with the attitude, "Oh well, I don't need to be concerned about refraining from sin, because God will bring good out of it anyway."

You might recall that such ideas aren't new. Even in the first century the concept was being tossed around as a logical conclusion to God's grace. That's why Paul wrote to the Romans, "What shall we say then? Are we to continue in sin so that grace may increase? May it never be! How shall we who died to sin still live in it?" (Romans 6:1–2).

No, our attitude can be such that we live in God's power to resist sin. But when we do sin, we can call upon the truth of Romans 8:28 to see God's promise fulfilled. To see what that could imply, let's look at this verse in a deeper way.

Going Deeper

The literal Greek language of Romans 8:28 says, "To the ones who love God He works together all things unto good." Let's look at this verse phrase by phrase to make sure we understand how we can apply its truths to diminish worry.

"To the ones who love God": Who does this apply to? Later in the verse it is clarified: "to them who are the called according to his purpose" (KJV). Every Christian is "called" and loves God to some degree. Could there be a connection between the degree of our love for God and our ability to trust Him? I believe so. The more we love God (which springs from our gratitude and knowledge of His wondrous nature), the more we trust Him. If you are having difficulty trusting God in the midst of the storms of life, look at your love for Him. If it is weak, learn more about His wonderful attributes: His love for you, His kindness, mercy, gentleness, power, and so many other endearing qualities.

"He works together": Spiros Zodhiates explains that in the Greek these two words connote "cooperate, contribute to an end or a goal."[2] God is orchestrating like a conductor the various aspects of our lives to fulfill His purposes and plans.

I think of that concept when I look at the underside of a tapestry. All the threads are jumbled and crisscrossed, seemingly without order or reason. But when the tapestry is turned over, I can see the beautiful design and what the craftsman had in mind. The same thing happens with the circumstances, struggles, problems, and challenges that we face. They all are "crafted" into making you and me more like Jesus and fulfilling God's plan in the world. You and I don't need to worry, even when we only see the underside of the tapestry of our lives.

"All things": All things means *all* things! The Greek word means *everything,* with nothing left out. It's all-inclusive of everything you and I experience. We can't pick and choose what we think God will use. Every worry, every fear, every circumstance and incident He works for good. God can even use our sin for His purposes.

When I was going through that time of abusing my daughter and hating my life, I thought, *Romans 8:28 certainly can't be true, because God can't possibly use my pitiful life for good.* But God *was* able to use even my sin for His glory and purposes. If you are discounting God's ability to use Romans 8:28 in your life because your worry is about a sinful habit, then look again! *Everything* can be used by God. God stands ready to help you overcome your sin. (Worry certainly doesn't help you do that.) So believe God wants to help you to have victory over your sin and your worry. Then look out for God's creativity in using it for His glory!

"Unto good": The Greek word for *good* means "something useful and profitable, beneficial."[3] *Vine's Expository Dictionary* defines it as "that which, being good in its character or constitution, is beneficial in its effect."[4] It's something good! Good is good! It's for our benefit. The potential worry itself is not necessarily good or beneficial, but what God brings out of it is good.

The "Good" of Cancer

About thirteen years ago my husband, Larry, and I faced a furious storm that threatened to drown us in its flood. It certainly didn't seem like it could be "good." Darcy, our daughter, was fifteen and a half and going through a rebellious time. She had begun talking regularly on the phone with a seventeen-year-old friend from school about his girlfriend. At times he would take Darcy out to talk about his problems. Before we knew it, Darcy had become the new girlfriend, even though she wasn't supposed to date until she turned sixteen.

Whenever Larry and I reminded her of our rule, she turned surly and argumentative. Every evening as she left she shouted at us, "You want to know why I'm leaving all the time? I hate being here. I can't wait until I turn eighteen. I'm outta here!"

I was stunned by her behavior. *Why is she so angry with us? What is going on in the relationship between this boy and Darcy? Is she staying true to the purity we taught her?* Time and again we tried to reach out to her. I felt worried and helpless because nothing seemed to make any difference. Each time we tried to talk to her she closed off emotionally and wouldn't respond.

That wasn't the only worry we were facing at that time. The biopsy of a mole on Larry's chest was diagnosed as melanoma—the deadliest kind of skin cancer. More tissue would have to be removed to determine if the cancer had gone inside his body. That struck a fearful chord within us, especially since a good friend of ours had died of melanoma three years earlier.

Is Larry's life in danger? Will I become a widow at such an early age? I prayed over and over again, *Lord God, I don't want to lose my best friend.*

God gave us a peace that we could trust His plan for Larry's life, yet I wasn't so sure about God's timing. *Lord, this will only push Darcy over the edge,* I cried. *She's already rebelling against you and us. She knows her daddy's life is in danger—this will just cause her to reject you even more. You don't know what you're doing!*

One evening Larry and I decided we had to try again to reach out to Darcy. Calling her into our bedroom, we asked her to sit in the chair while we sat against the headboard on our bed. As soon as Darcy sat down she crossed her arms and glared at us, seemingly defying us to break through her cold and distant veneer.

"Darcy, honey, we love you," Larry began. "We want to know what's going on so that we can work through our differences."

Darcy sat immobilized, her face just as impassive as ever. I spoke up, "Darcy, we really do want to talk this out. We love and care about you. Please let us know how you're feeling and what the problem is."

Darcy still sat silent, her lips pursed in defiance.

Larry and I looked at each other, feeling hopeless and helpless. *O God,* I prayed silently, *please help us. What will get through to her?*

Larry and I continued to try to reason with Darcy. Then without any explanation, her face softened, her arms came down, and she began talking to us. We were thrilled! For forty-five minutes we talked and talked. We found out she wanted to keep a pure relationship with her boyfriend and that her values were similar to ours. As we all talked, Larry and I shot glances at each other, silently asking, *Why is she finally talking to us?* We had no idea.

When we were finished, Darcy stood up and walked over to the bedroom door. She put her hand on the knob, opened the door slightly, and then hesitated. She looked back at us with a confused look and said, "I don't know why I'm talking to you like this—" Then, as if the reason had just occurred to her, she continued, "but it's because Daddy has cancer."

God healed our relationship through something that we thought could never be used for good: cancer. As strong-willed as she was, the Lord knew that only something as severe as possibly losing her daddy would make Darcy see life from a different perspective.

She never returned to that state of rebellion, and today we all have a fantastic relationship. She is a married woman who loves God. We rejoice that Larry has been free of melanoma since then. God knows how to work in people's lives, and we've seen that to be true in our family.

Are there dark clouds off in your future? Does it seem like a storm is a-comin'? Even if the storm arrives, bringing lots of lightning and thunder with it, God has a plan for turning the storm into a blessing . . . with a rainbow in the clouds.

Jochebed / EXODUS 2

Jochebed had a lot to worry about. She had given birth to a son. Normally a wonderful joy, it was like a death knell to the family because Pharaoh had ordered that all sons born to the Hebrew people be killed. Jochebed must have been on pins and needles caring for the child for three months after his birth. If he cried she had to shush him, lest someone hear him. When she nursed him and he made gurgling sounds of satisfaction, could she whisper her love without fearing someone would hear her? How about the other Hebrew women whose sons had been killed? Did she fear that they would report her out of their own jealousy and grief?

She must have looked over her shoulder a thousand times, wondering who was watching her as she took care of Moses and brought him out of his hiding place to nurse him and care for him. And it wasn't for Moses' sake alone that she feared; in disobeying the Pharaoh, her own life was in danger. A double worry!

Edith Deen muses, "How Jochebed managed to save her son from Pharaoh's edict during the first three months of Moses' life is not recorded. We can imagine she might have hidden him in a donkey stable or a storage room where she kept clay jars filled with grain, peppercorns, onions, bread, dates, and other foods. But after he became three months old, she knew she could no longer take the risk of hiding him."[5]

If we didn't know the end of the story, we might be biting our fingernails, wondering and fretting, *What will happen to Moses?* Without her faith in God, Jochebed wouldn't have had the courage to hide him. Even *with* her faith in God, she must have been afraid to send him floating on the Nile River with no guarantee of the child's protection. As she planned to prepare a basket for her little bundle of joy, I can only imagine the fearful thoughts swirling in her mind:

I just know he'll wiggle and cry. The basket will tip over and he'll be drowned.

I just know he'll be discovered by a soldier who will kill him immediately.

I just know the river will sweep him downstream, and we'll never know what happened to him.

I just know the princess will call the soldiers to have Moses killed.

I just know the crocodiles will eat him.

I just know . . .

Did Jochebed have such thoughts? Most mothers would have, yet she must have felt God was guiding her to make such a bold move. She didn't just worry, wonder, and fret; she took action as God led.

We know God brought good things out of her obedience—a

deliverer for the Israelites, and the founding of a great nation. We want to be like Jochebed, and we can be!

 ## DISCUSSION QUESTIONS

1. What are you worried about the most right now? How does that fear make you feel?

2. Do you agree that worry is a sin? If not, why not? If you do, why?

3. In what ways do you see how worry becomes a "distraction"?

4. What physical or mental reactions within you indicate that you are worrying?

5. What destructive responses and physical problems have you seen as a result of worry—both in yourself and in others? What do you think God's attitude is about those consequences of worry?

6. Can you share a time when Romans 8:28 helped you not to worry? Did the thing you were worried about actually happen?

7. How often would you estimate that what you worry about actually happens?

8. Read Exodus 2. What do you find most amazing about Jochebed's story?

9. What good things did God bring about through Jochebed's faith and resistance to worry? (Exodus 2:7–10). List them by verse:

   Verses 7–8:

   Verse 9:

   Verse 10:

10. From what you know about the story of Moses' life, how else did God bring good from Jochebed's trust?

11. In what way will you fight worry this next week? Can you put

your worry into perspective by asking yourself, "What is the worst thing that could happen?" and then think of how God could use it for good?

Letter from God

My Precious Daughter,

I understand that life can bring many worries. I never intended that life be free of problems, only that the problems would draw you closer to My loving heart. If you didn't experience difficulty, you would have no need of Me. I want you to need Me so that we can grow more intimate and you can depend upon Me more and more.

Jochebed learned that by doing the very thing that she feared. She trusted that I knew what I was doing and would bring good from it. Of course she felt fearful. I understand your feelings. I created you with emotions, so don't think I'm shocked by your fear. But I do want you to trust in Me and not allow fear to become worry. Turn your cares over to Me. You really have nothing to worry about. Nothing!

Can you trust that I know best and want only the best for you? Worry hurts you and has no influence whatsoever upon My plan or will. I love you and don't want you to suffer the consequences of worry. I've given you the promise that I can use everything for good. Please trust Me. I can see the end from the beginning and how I plan to work. You are so very, very important to Me. I don't plan anything for your harm, only your good.

Keep My promises in mind and turn your problems and difficulties over to Me. You can trust Me.

I love you.

Your Heavenly Father

CHAPTER 2

Walking on the *Sunny Side*

Perfect Love Casts Out Fear

When Larry and I began considering his retirement, the desert was the last place I thought we'd settle. I always considered it a dusty and dirty place, too hot in the summer and too cold in the winter. Yet when visiting friends who lived in the desert, we found it to be a rather appealing location. When we made the decision to move here, I wondered, *It's such a huge change from the Los Angeles area; will we like it? How will I survive the hot summers? I've lived in the same house for thirty-three years; will I enjoy our new home as much?*

I shouldn't have worried. We have loved the area and the weather, since there are many more months of perfect weather than uncomfortable ones. Lots of sunshine graces each day with crystal-clear skies, revealing bright orange sunrises and magnificent sunsets dotted by multicolored hot air balloons floating toward us.

The abundance of sun and a natural underground aquifer (a water-bearing bed of rock or gravel) provide the perfect combination for growing lush plants and colorful desert flora. What I'd never realized before was how colorful desert plants are. Most desert plants bloom with flowers in purples, reds, and oranges. Purple seems to be the most popular of God's desert creations, and I thought, *How appropriate from a royal King of Kings. It's the color of royalty.*

With all the beauty and clear skies, I sometimes take it all for granted. I can get so wrapped up in duties and responsibilities in the house that when Larry calls, "Kath, you've got to come see this magnificent sunset," I'm tempted to respond, "Oh, just a minute, I've got to finish making dinner." Of course, by the time I've finished dinner, the beauty of the sunset is gone and the sun has disappeared behind the mountains. Then I mentally kick myself for missing a part of our day that we enjoy together. But when I choose to leave my cooking or come away from my desk, I'm reminded again of the blessings we enjoy here.

I'm also reminded that I was initially worried whether we were making the right decision to move here. I needn't have worried. God guided us in His love to enjoy this place of beauty and sunshine. It's another life experience of learning not to worry, to think of the sun representing the "Son-shine" of God's love. Sadly, even His love is something that I can take for granted, just like the beauty the desert offers. But when I'm diligent to remind myself of God's love, I realize I can worry less because He has only good intentions for me. Let's look at three principles that will help us live in the "Son-shine" of God's love:

- God is pure love.
- God is perfect love.
- God is prudent love.

God Is Pure Love

The Bible says, "The one who does not love does not know God, for God is love" (1 John 4:8). You can ask just about anyone, "Is God loving?" and they'll most likely answer, "Of course!" But inside that very person is often lurking the question, "But if God really is love, He wouldn't have . . ." And then the list could include any number of things:

- allowed my child to die;
- allowed my husband to walk out on me;

- allowed that man to rape me;
- allowed that automobile accident that has given me pain ever since.

That's how we justify worry. We reason, *If God is love and He allowed those hurtful things, then maybe He can't be trusted with this "something" I'm worried about. I still have to be in charge of this situation, because God isn't really trustworthy. Maybe my worry will prevent something bad from happening.*

We often have these feelings because our definition of "good" is skewed as it becomes influenced by society. Love, by the world's definition, is a romantic kind of thing that we fall into and can just as easily fall out of. "Reality Romance" television programs such as *The Bachelor* or *The Bachelorette* communicate that we must be beautiful and have a fabulous body in order to earn love. We might find ourselves believing an example of love can be found in watching celebrity couples. When those couples break up, we find ourselves getting nervous. *If they can't remain in love, surrounded by wealth and comfort, how can I?* We ask, *Can my husband want the best for me for many years?* or *Can God really be trusted to want the best for me?*

We must answer loud and clear, "No, I'm not guaranteed a forever kind of love with my husband/boyfriend, but I can depend upon God's love because He is purely interested in my best."

Many years ago I heard Winkie Pratney, an evangelist from New Zealand, say, "Love is a choice for a person's highest good." That is God's kind of love—pure. He wants only the best for us, and only He knows what is the best for us.

If we are worried that He'll withhold something from us that we believe will make us happy, we can be confident that if He doesn't give it to us, it's for our best. If we are worried that He'll allow something in our lives that we believe will make us unhappy, we can be confident that if He allows it, it's only for our best. (In chapter 6 we'll explore the purpose of troubles more deeply.)

I can remember a time when God withheld something from me that I believed would be for my best. I felt snubbed. It's one of those experiences where you look back and think, *I'm sure glad He didn't answer yes to that prayer!*

Remember when I described in chapter 1 about my being so angry with Larry? We had been married for seven years and were like married singles. I was terrified that our marriage would end in divorce and that I would kill our daughter in one of my rages. In my worry and fear, I tried to get my needs met in whatever selfish way I could. In my desperation to have Larry love me and meet my needs, I prayed, "God, cause him to be in an accident where he'll get hurt and become a paraplegic."

As I look back, I'm absolutely astounded by my sick logic. I was grasping for any straw to prevent my worst fear: that we would get a divorce. So I rationalized that if Larry were injured, he would have to stay home and couldn't run off working two jobs and flying an airplane.

The scary thing is that I was serious. It made perfect sense to me, clouded as my mind was by my fear. This was the way I would get love; certainly God would see it my way. His love for me would guarantee a positive answer! Obviously, I couldn't even see that having a paralyzed husband would bring tremendous responsibilities and difficulties to our lives and that it would not give me the love I hungered for. I definitely wasn't living in the "Son-shine" of God's love.

Of course, I'm really glad now that God turned me down on that selfish prayer. He healed our marriage in His own way, without injuring Larry, and today I'm not taking care of a paralyzed man!

Worry clouds our thinking and gives us a warped definition of love. But God always knows what's best for us. He is love—pure love that never selfishly demands His own way but wants only the very best for each of us . . . for you! You can resist worry because you can live in the knowledge that God loves you. Live like God loves you *purely*—what a great way to resist worry!

God Is Perfect Love

One afternoon, after I'd been a Christian for about five years, I drove home from church feeling downhearted. *Why can't I love God enough?* I asked myself over and over again. I was afraid that if I didn't love him "enough," He would never fully accept me as His child. I remembered 1 John 4:18, and it seemed to scream of my need to have a perfect love toward God: "There is no fear in love; but perfect love casts out fear."

If your love for God was perfect, you wouldn't have any fear of Him and you wouldn't ever worry! I berated myself. *Lord, it's just hopeless. I can never love you enough to take away this fear of what you might do to me if I don't measure up.*

Then the real meaning of that verse broke open in my heart and mind like the sun bursting forth from behind a black cloud. *Wait a minute, Lord! That verse isn't talking about my love for you, but your love for me. Now I understand. Your perfect love can cast out my fear because you want what's best for me. Oh, thank you!*

Years later I identified why I had misinterpreted 1 John 4:18. My perfectionistic tendencies believed that I needed to become perfect in order for God to love me. I find that many women suffer from the same thing. They can't believe they can be free of worry since they haven't performed perfectly—or even close to it. They believe they are not worthy of God's love or the goodness He desires for them.

In my book *Why Do I Put So Much Pressure on Myself and Others?*[1] I relate how perfectionism can steal our ability to believe God loves us. I include a quiz to help women identify to what degree they are perfectionists. As you read the following statements, check any that are true of you, even if it is true only some of the time.

1. _____ Most of the time I sense God is disappointed with me.
2. _____ I spend lots of energy evaluating my performance.
3. _____ I tend to think in terms of "all or nothing."
4. _____ I think I should have my act together by now.
5. _____ My expectations tend to be unrealistic.
6. _____ For me, "good" is rarely "good enough."
7. _____ I often wonder why other people can't get their act together.
8. _____ I'm compelled to straighten out misunderstandings.
9. _____ I won't begin something if there's a possibility I can't do it well.

Now add up your check marks for your score.

Score: _____

If you checked three or more statements you have perfectionist tendencies. Someone has said that a perfectionist is a person who takes great pains . . . and passes them on to others. And a perfectionist has a hard time receiving God's love. Let's examine why that's true.

When we have perfectionist tendencies, we have a mindset that says, "I haven't achieved perfection, or anything close to it, and since God must be upset about that, I better worry, because He can't possibly want my best!"

My friend and fellow writer Kat Dunkle relates to that. She told me,

> Within a short ninety-day period when I was in my twenties, our eight-year-old son was hit by a car and died, my father died of a heart attack, we lost our business to bankruptcy, and I was in an accident that left me clinically dead on the operating table.
>
> Following all these events I lost my ability to trust anyone, including God. I fought with my husband constantly and was so fearful of my two remaining sons' lives that I obsessively protected them. I pushed them to the limit to be the best in sports and school. I started a business and became very successful, all proving that I could do it on my own.
>
> Yet God was working more strongly than my perfectionism! During the surgery for the accident that left me clinically dead, I had an experience with God that's difficult to explain. He brought me back to life, and I turned from being an agnostic to seeking God. I was not yet a committed believer, but God's intervention started me on the road to finding Him.
>
> In the beginning, my perfectionism was stronger than my faith, but little by little, over many years, my trust in God became stronger than my perfectionism. I began releasing control over my sons, my husband, and my own life. The Bible became my everyday companion. I underlined all the wonderful words God had just for me. I couldn't stop praying.
>
> I'm finding that releasing my perfectionism and replacing it with trust in God's perfect love is an ongoing process that is enhanced by staying in God's Word even when I don't "feel" like it. When fear or worry creep back into my life—and they do—I turn to my Bible, prayer, and godly friends for support.

If fear is creating perfectionist tendencies or reactions in you, dear reader, then learn from Kat Dunkle. God's love for you is *perfect*, not requiring your perfection. All that's required is His faithfulness. Enjoy the "Son-shine" of God's love. Live like God loves you *perfectly*—then there's no room for worry!

God Is Prudent Love

Dee e-mailed me recently and shared this story about her own struggle with worry and her victory over it.

> Last week the "What if" monster came to haunt me. His mouth gaped, exposing sharp teeth as he salivated, growled, and threatened me. A good friend had asked me to go to breakfast at a local restaurant. The last time we ate there I ran into someone who had hurt me in the past. I feared I'd see him again, even though it's been five years since the Lord helped me to forgive him.
>
> I prayed, "Lord, why can't I seem to overcome this fearful monster, which repeatedly spews, *WHAT IF you see him again? WHAT IF he hurts you again? WHAT IF . . . ? WHAT IF . . . ?*" The Lord immediately reminded me of what He has done. "I delivered you from that hurt. My love will protect you. I am your Vindicator. What can man possibly do to you? Trust in Me. Believe in Me. I am there with you."
>
> I had to ask myself, *Who am I going to believe? The lies from this pestering monster or the truth from the mouth of God?* I realized it's very easy to find a Scripture and quickly "claim" it . . . to say it over and over again, as if the words themselves will send the bad monster running. Is my faith in the words or is it in the One who spoke them?
>
> Lately I have been fighting worry by spending more and more time in God's presence, experiencing His tenderness and grace. As I open His Word and open my heart, He begins to reveal himself to me. This takes His timing. There is no quick antidote to overcome fear. I went to that breakfast meeting in complete peace.

Dee is successfully fighting worry by living out the truths of 1 Peter 5:6–9:

Therefore humble yourselves under the mighty hand of God, that He may exalt you at the proper time, casting all your anxiety on Him, because He cares for you. Be of sober spirit, be on the alert. Your adversary, the devil, prowls around like a roaring lion, seeking someone to devour. But resist him, firm in your faith, knowing that the same experiences of suffering are being accomplished by your brethren who are in the world.

God is ready and wise as He responds to us. We can cast our anxiety upon Him because He cares about us so very much. In fact, you are the *object* of His interest! That's why I've entitled this section "God Is Prudent Love." The word *prudent* means "capable of exercising sound judgment in practical matters, especially as concerns one's own interests."[2]

Learning to Cast Our Care

God wants us to *cast* all our anxiety upon Him. *Cast* is a Greek word that denotes violence! Surprised? I was! Previously, I'd envisioned the word *cast* as referring to a fly fisherman calmly casting his lure out over an ambling stream with the bright sun shining and birds twittering in the background. But girl, that isn't the picture of this word *cast*.

The Greek word is more synonymous with words like *hurling, thrusting, expelling,* and *throwing.* Imagine a baseball pitcher hurling that ball so fast that we can't even see it on TV—that's how we're supposed to cast our worries upon Him. We're supposed to take quick action! My friend and neighbor Joanie Dill told me her definition of worry: "stewing without doing." If we will cast our worry on God, we won't be guilty of that!

I recently talked with a woman named Cherie at a retreat in the Midwest, and she gave me an example of casting. Cherie and her husband, Gene, were deeply concerned about their eighteen-year-old daughter and her boyfriend. Mallory and Noah had been dating for about two months, but already Cherie and Gene sensed "red flags" about this young man. Noah frequently threw around one-hundred-dollar bills as if they were candy bars. He bought Mallory expensive gifts and seemed eager to show his bulging wallet.

When Cherie and Gene tried to point out to her how unusual it was for a nineteen-year-old to have hundreds of dollars available, she reasoned, "His parents own a construction company, and they pay him well." Cherie and Gene smelled something suspicious, but reasoning with Mallory didn't seem to make any difference.

Cherie and Gene finally took action, forbidding Mallory to receive any more gifts from Noah, even as they cast their worry upon God in prayer, asking Him to take action on Mallory's behalf.

Then Noah was in an automobile accident, and drugs were found in his car when the police arrived. Though he was under the influence of drugs, he claimed he was carrying the drugs for someone else. Mallory's eyes were opened. With a sigh of relief and thanks to God, Cherie and Gene saw their daughter willing to break off her relationship with Noah. They had wisely taken appropriate action when it was called for, even as they took their concern to God in prayer.

Right now my mind keeps being pulled away from my task at hand because a repairman is coming to repair the toilets in our house. I've told myself, "I'll clean the toilets after I write for one hour," but I wonder, *Will he come early because one of the other homeowners he's calling on won't be there?*

Anxiety and worry seek to divide and conquer, making us unable to focus and fight against our worry. Taking action along with trusting God are the keys that 1 Peter 5:7 give us. So I'm going to take action in my casting . . . excuse me while I go make my bed and clean the toilets.

Okay . . . I'm back. Did I miss anything? Now I'm at peace. I took the necessary action even while trusting God that the time spent away from this chapter could be redeemed. Let's continue looking at Peter's words, where he writes, "Your adversary, the devil, prowls around like a roaring lion, seeking someone to devour." He writes those words immediately after giving us a big exhortation to trust God.

We can easily see that Satan wants to defeat us by keeping us worried—that way, we are pitiful representatives of the kingdom. We lose our confidence and we shamefully hide from expressing our trust in God to others. Most of us don't really take Satan very seriously; after all, we think, *Who am I that Satan would earmark me for attention?*

But each warrior in God's army is important, and Satan isn't selective in who he wants to subvert. He'll take me, and you!

The Power of God's Word

We can fight him through the power of God's Word. When worry assails me, I begin to mull the fear over and over. Even when I identify it as worry, and sometimes even when I turn it over to the Lord, the fears still haunt me. But victory comes from the truth in Revelation 12:10–11:

> Then I heard a loud voice in heaven, saying, "Now the salvation, and the power, and the kingdom of our God and the authority of His Christ have come, for the *accuser* of our brethren has been thrown down, he who accuses them before our God day and night. And they overcame him because of the blood of the Lamb and because of the word of their testimony, and they did not love their life even when faced with death" (italics added).

I apply these verses by rebuking Satan out loud (and sometimes it's loud!), saying something like: "Satan, in the name of Jesus and through the blood that Jesus shed for me, I tell you to leave me alone! You're not going to accuse and hassle me anymore about this worry. I trust God for it! Get away from me!"

Invariably, several minutes later I mentally "wake up" and think, "Hey, wasn't I worried about something a short time ago? I can't remember what it was!" Or if I remember what it was, the confusion or anxiety over it is no longer there. Peace has begun to reign in my heart.

This is a powerful promise from God that we need to use. In fact, why don't you practice it right now? Unless someone is going to stare at you (and even if they are—who cares?) say out loud what I wrote about rebuking Satan. You can, of course, form your own wording, but remember to rebuke and resist Satan through the blood of the Lamb and your testimony (which means reviewing how God has helped you in the past). I guarantee that whatever you were worried about will either lose its anxious power over you or you won't even remember what you were so worried about!

Verda Glick tells in her book *Deliver the Ransom Alone* about a trial that summoned all of her ability to trust God and resist Satan's temptation to worry. She and her husband, Eli, are missionaries in El Salvador and have been victims of numerous armed robberies. One day she heard her oldest son's pickup in their driveway. Taking his mother into his arms, Ernest told her, "Mama, robbers kept Papa on the mountain. They're asking for ransom. Come, sit down." Her greatest fear had come about.

Eli had gone as usual to hold a weekly preaching service at El Paste, a mountain in western El Salvador. Ernest explained that bandits had captured Eli and the twenty-four persons who had gone with him. When the kidnappers released the group, they told the driver, "We will keep the pastor. Tell his wife to send us $11,500. His oldest son must deliver the ransom alone. If he's not here with the money by two o'clock tomorrow afternoon, we'll kill our captive."

Verda's knees felt weak and tightness constricted her chest. "Oh, son," she stammered, "let's pray." They fell on their knees by the old brown sofa and asked God for wisdom to know what to do. For the first time, the roles of mother and son were reversed. Verda wept on her son's chest and he wrapped his arms around her, reassuring her.

But her thoughts warred with letting her son deliver the ransom. "How can I let Ernest go up that mountain alone? I need him. He's more mature than I've ever seen him before. I want him here with me." Verda's love for Eli made her want to pay the ransom quickly, but her love for Ernest made her want to hold him back. She felt torn between her love for each of them.

After an agony of indecision, Verda knew she must send Ernest to deliver the ransom, which a local hardware merchant loaned them. After weeping in his arms once more and kissing him good-bye, she let him carry the big package of money to the pickup and drive away. With a troubled heart she turned to the One who sent His only Son to deliver the ransom for her. She says, "My heavenly Father, who didn't spare His own Son from that dangerous mission, now filled me with strength and peace while my son went on his. Hours later, both my husband and son returned home safely. I have a deeper appreciation now for the love that compelled God to send His Son to deliver the ransom for me. That love sustained me in one of the most difficult situations I have ever faced."[3]

Verda learned in a powerful way about God's love, a love so great that God sent His precious Son, Jesus, to die on the cross for your sins and mine. How can we not trust that kind of love? As we focus on Jesus, the "Son-shine" of our lives, and don't take for granted our heavenly Father's caring love, we'll be assured that He wants what is best and good for us. We *can* trust God knowing that His love is pure, perfect, and prudent.

Rebekah / GENESIS 25:20–34; 27:1–46

Rebekah had a lot to worry about. Before her twin sons were born, God told her, "Two nations are in your womb; and two peoples will be separated from your body; and one people shall be stronger than the other; and the older shall serve the younger" (Genesis 25:23).

When they were grown, Rebekah hatched a plan to make sure that the younger son, Jacob, would get the inheritance rather than the older one, Esau. God had said it would be fulfilled, but when it appeared that it wouldn't, Rebekah couldn't trust God and forced it to happen her way. Because Esau was swindled out of his inheritance, he threatened his brother's life. Then Rebekah took matters into her own hands, *again*! She encouraged her husband, Isaac, to send Jacob away to her brother's home to visit, thinking he could return soon (Genesis 27:41–45).

We can only imagine the worry that consumed her as she fretted over her favorite son, Jacob. Maybe it played out something like this:

Rebekah paced across the rugs on the dirt floor of the tent. "Oh, my, oh, my! What can I do? Esau is going to kill Jacob. I just know it!" She stopped wringing her hands long enough to peek out through the flap in the tent, fully expecting to see Jacob stumbling up to her, blood pouring from a knife in his chest, saying, "Esau stabbed me! Help me, Mother!"

"Oh, no! Oh, no! O Jehovah, you got us into this mess when you said Esau would serve Jacob. Why did you do that? Can't you see the problems it has made? Well, I'll just have to take care of this. What can I do?"

Rebekah continued to pace and wring her hands until she slashed a cut in her hand with one of her fingernails. She drew the blood, trying to make the wound close up, when the thought suddenly popped into her brain. "That's it! I'll send Jacob to my brother's house! That'll keep him out of harm's way, and then he can come home as soon as Esau's anger cools. Oh, I'm so glad I thought of it! This will solve all our problems!"

We shake our heads in dismay, because Rebekah's manipulations didn't solve anything. What happened wasn't God's original plan, but He certainly ended up using it. The saddest thing, though, is that Rebekah never saw her beloved son again. He stayed at her brother's house for many years, and she died before he returned. We can only imagine the loneliness and sadness she experienced in those years of waiting for him. Her worry had stolen from her the very thing she tried to protect: her son's presence.

Rebekah wasn't able to trust God's love for her. We don't want to be like that, and we don't have to be!

 ## DISCUSSION QUESTIONS

1. What is your definition of love?

2. What strikes you when you read 1 John 4:8?

3. Do you have an ending to "But if God really is love, He wouldn't have. . . ."?

4. How do you think the world influences people's definition of love?

5. To what prayer of yours did God not answer yes (and now you're glad He refused your request)?

6. Read 1 John 4:18. What is important to you in this verse?

7. What did you score on the perfectionist quiz? Did you see any

perfectionist tendencies that might be fueling your worry?

8. How would you like to actively cast your current worry into God's loving hands?

9. To what degree would you say you have identified the spiritual attack you are under when you begin to worry? What do you plan to do about it?

10. What impresses or disappoints you about Rebekah's story? How do you think you would have acted in a similar situation?

11. Memorize one of the verses this chapter covers.

Letter from God

My Precious Daughter,

My love for you is so much greater than you will ever know; not until you reach heaven will you fully understand it. I know that you can't fully comprehend now how much I love you, but I do want you to grow more confident of My love for you. The more you know and feel My love, the more you'll be able to trust Me! I want that because I know it's for your good and your benefit.

I'm the only one who knows what the definition of benefit *is for you. It's a unique plan and desire for you that can't be compared to that of anyone else. It comes out of My intimate knowledge of you. I fashion the tapestry of your life so that every thread is designed to draw you closer to My loving passion for you. Don't just look at the jumbled threads on the back; look at the beautiful reflection of Me that I am working on the front. Even other people are noticing the work I'm doing in you. Rejoice! My love can be trusted.*

Enjoy the sunshine of My love.

Your Heavenly Father

CHAPTER 3

Catching the *Rainbow*

How Prayer Alleviates Worry

I quickly dialed my son's cell phone number from my cell phone. "Can you see that? Isn't it magnificent? Do you have your camera ready?"

Larry and I were headed to his parents' home to visit for Easter, and our twenty-one-year-old son, Mark, was driving his pickup truck a short distance behind us. He couldn't stay the total time we were visiting so he was driving separately.

Mark had already seen what I was talking about—a huge double rainbow—that filled the sky in front of us, touching down on both sides. I'd never seen such a beautiful display of a rainbow, and evidently Mark had not either, because he replied, "I'm pulling over right now to take a photo. I hope it comes out great!" Mark is a freelance photographer, so I knew the shot would be an attractive one to him.

Later, doing some research on rainbows, I found out some interesting facts. A rainbow is a pattern of reflected light and, as all of us know, they can't occur without rain. What I didn't know, before my research, is that when you see a rainbow, you are at the center of it. If someone else is looking at the very same rainbow, even if they are a mile away, they are also at the center of it. Thus, we each see a different view of that rainbow.

God created the rainbow after the global flood as a visual reminder to Noah of His promise—that He would never destroy the earth by flood again (Genesis 9:12–17). The storm that created the flood was the first storm on earth, so Noah had never encountered a storm before that. When the next storm came, Noah must have worried, *Will it flood the earth again?* Yet when he saw the rainbow in the sky, he remembered God's promise. He must have sighed, *Ahhh, that's right. God promised.*

As the rainbow was Noah's connection with God's promises, prayer is yours and mine. Whenever you are assailed by the storms of worry, you can lay hold of prayer, which could be called the "rainbow" of God's promises. He wants us to come to Him, talk to Him, and leave our concerns, worries, and fears with Him. And as we pray He will direct us in any action that He wants us to take. That's why we must: Pray! Stay! Obey!

Pray!

Prayer is what most people think of as the solution to worry. And they are right! That's why Philippians 4:6 is so essential in our study of worry. It says, "Be anxious for nothing, but in everything by prayer and supplication with thanksgiving let your requests be made known to God."

In *The Message* that verse is translated, "Don't fret or worry. Instead of worrying, pray. Let petitions and praises shape your worries into prayers, letting God know your concerns."

Now, before you get worried, let me assure you that we will also study the next most famous verse for dealing with worry, which is verse 7. We will study that verse in the next chapter and we're also going to save the concept of verse 6 about "thanksgiving" for that chapter. After all, once we experience the storm, we'll need to pull out the umbrella to protect us. We'll find out how the "umbrella" of gratitude, among other things, strengthens us to have victory over worry.

What impresses me the most when I read Philippians 4:6 is how it stresses the words *nothing* and *everything*. *Absolutely nothing* needs be worried about and absolutely *everything* can be brought to God in prayer.

But my natural reaction when I don't have control is to think, *Now, this deserves to be worried about!* Be honest. Haven't you thought that too? There are just some things—even if God is powerful enough, even if God cares enough, even if God loves me enough—that are worthy of being worried about!

Unfortunately, Satan's lie is "God helps those who help themselves." During my childhood I got the impression that I should take care of the little worries and let God take care of the big ones. After all, there was so much that God had on His mind, why bother Him about the things that I could handle? The problem was that I didn't handle even the little worries very well, but I still felt I should keep them on my plate.

Philippians 4:6 dispels this lie. God wants us to take *everything* to Him, every little and big thing—no exceptions. But there's a strange satisfaction we can get while we're worrying that encourages us to keep worries and concerns close at hand. It's this: Worrying feels good! Worrying made me feel like I was the center of the universe. It's a very selfish, self-centered occupation. After all, when I'm worried I'm wondering what is going to happen to *me*. (And if I'm worried about *you*, I'm wondering what is going to happen to you that will affect *me*.)

To counteract that, God wants us to feel like we're at the center— not of the universe, but—of His thoughts when we pray, just as you and I are always looking at the center of a rainbow. Let Rev. James Snyder's remarks delight you and make the same point. He shared with me in an e-mail,

> There is nothing more satisfying than a good session of worrying. Yes, I said worrying. Nothing is more delectable than getting into a good stew. The reason worrying has received such a bad rap is that too many amateurs get involved. Believe me; true worrying is nothing to fool around with. It's only for those who have achieved some semblance of expertise. It takes years of diligent practice to arrive at a level of accomplishment, and few people reach it.

Through the years, I have found that my expertise in the fine art of worrying has benefited me. I must admit I have worried from time to time that I did not have enough experience for the really big things. I know what some people say about this. I have heard it all my life. They tell me that 90 percent of what I worry about never happens. This has never upset me, because my worrying was responsible for that 90 percent not happening. I can hardly imagine what life would have been like had I not worried some of those things away.

When I can't sleep at night, instead of tossing and turning like many folks do, I spend the time worrying about something. There is always something to worry about. If I cannot think of something, I can always worry about that. Some count sheep; I worry about whether they are feeding the sheep enough, how their wool is coming along this year, and how much the shepherd will get for their wool. This art of worrying has been a great thing for me.

For example, when I am at the airport I worry. A lot. I look around and see so many people reading a book or working on laptop computers or talking on their cell phones. What a waste of good worrying time. The first thing I see when I walk into an airport is a big sign that says, "Terminal." That sign alone is good for two hours of hard worrying. Each time I go to the airport and see that sign, I find new depths of worrying. A novice would not know what to worry about or where to begin.

There is another side to all this. I can keep on worrying or I can start practicing a life of prayer. I can either worry or trust. I cannot do both at the same time.

I trust Rev. Snyder's writing brings a smile to your face. By the way, do you know how useful humor can be in diminishing worry? The next time you're worried, force yourself to smile. I guarantee you'll feel the load of worry lighten.

Rev. Snyder has also highlighted another very important point: We can't worry and trust at the same time. If we choose to pray, thus turning our attention to the Lord, worry can't inhabit our thoughts as easily.

That word *choice* is crucial. Praying is a choice! It is a conscious decision to turn our minds from worry to God's ability to deliver us, help us, or guide us. It's a hard choice because we can easily believe lies like "worry feels good," "it works," or "it is necessary." But by making the choice to turn our minds toward trusting God, we will find it easier and easier to do as time goes on. Let me make some suggestions for choosing prayer:

- *Prayer can be fast or slow.* When the storms of life threaten or the weather isn't cooperating with your plans, look for the rainbow. An arrow prayer can be as short as *Lord, help—I'm worried about this! I'm not going to rehearse what I think could go badly. I'm going to believe you'll take care of this situation.*

When we later have the opportunity to spend more time with God, we can spend more concentrated energy focusing on whatever is bothering us and trying to steal our peace. Ideally, we should spend extended time with God several times a week—even more often if possible.

- *Use your journal.* My journal becomes my cure for worry as I pour out my concerns to God and write out my prayers. I also find my old journals a great breeding ground for trust in God as I realize that what I was worried about then (and it seemed like the end of the world), God solved. Often I think, *You mean I was worried about that? How could that have seemed so important?*

Some women have a hard time using a journal because they believe they must record their thoughts perfectly. Let me assure you that your journal writing doesn't have to be perfectly written. Simply express the cries of your heart and soul. It is your tool for getting in touch with your heart for God. It doesn't have to be ready to publish!

- *List all your worries.* Turn this list into a prayer list as you write a prayer about each one. And add a Scripture to go along with it.
- *Pray with someone else about your worry.* Be careful not to go on and on about the worry, but quickly turn to God, committing it to Him.
- *Choose a "worry time"—with a twist.* Now this one is going to seem like a strange suggestion, but it works! Throughout your day, when worries rise up, tell yourself, "I won't worry about that now,

I'll save it for my 'worry time.'" Then pick a time to worry but with this twist: Write out each thing that you're worried about and counter it with trust in God, with the truth (corrected thinking) and/or a Bible verse. But only give yourself ten minutes to actually "worry." Turn on the timer, and when the bell goes off, you must stop! Close the session in prayer. And if you're afraid you'll go beyond your ten minutes, ask a friend to call you at the end of your time to hold you accountable.

- *Do whatever God tells you to do.* Yes, some worries don't have solutions and we are not supposed to respond to them (for instance, if a situation isn't our responsibility). But often there *is* something we can do, and God wants to guide us to do the right thing.

Janet Lynn Mitchell (coauthor of *A Special Kind of Love: For Those Who Love Children With Special Needs*) found that praying and doing go together! Here's what she shared with me. She had borrowed her grandmother's good dishes from her mother to prepare a meal for the gathering after the funeral of her friend Annette's mother. About a week after the funeral, Janet called Annette to offer to pick up the dishes and return them to her mother. Janet was shocked when Annette said, "Janet, I dropped them off the day after the funeral. You weren't home so I set them behind the plants by your front door."

Janet rushed to the front door but the dishes weren't there. She sadly told her friend, and they decided to pray for a week, asking God to somehow return the dishes before Janet told her mother the sad news. Even though Janet continued to check by the front porch bushes, nothing appeared, and finally Janet told her mom. Her mom was also sad but handled it well.

Janet explains,

The following week I drove into our neighborhood and noticed an elderly woman walking down the sidewalk. God seemed to whisper, *Janet, stop and ask this women if she has seen your dishes!*

Immediately I pulled over and said to the woman, "Excuse me, ma'am, but I'm wondering if perhaps you've seen some dishes. I live around the corner and a friend put some dishes on my front porch. These dishes were my grandma's and a family treasure . . . and now they are missing." But the woman only said, "No English."

That night when I returned from a meeting, my husband said, "An elderly woman knocked on our door. When I opened it, she said, 'No English.' Then she handed me these bags." Inside the bags were my grandma's dishes. I was so grateful that I prayed and then followed God's directions!

The next time you are worried, pray! If you're not able to spend some time praying right then, offer up an arrow prayer and concentrate on it later. Find out whether God wants you to release the care to Him or take action.

Stay!

Once we make that decision to turn our worry over to God in prayer, guess what's going to happen? You know it already—we are tempted to take back the worry! We say, "Lord, I can't do anything about this, and I believe You're going to handle it. It's Yours." Moments later we look back at the dark storm clouds, take our eyes off the rainbow, and things look bleak again.

Didn't I just turn that over to God? I truly meant it and I truly believed it. Why is it hounding me again? That is the nature of our minds. We can easily take back the worry. Like a puppy who is being trained to "stay!" we waggle our tail of worry and scamper away from trusting God.

Well, there's another part of prayer: staying power! We will most often need to pray and then *keep* praying, because Satan wants us to change our focus back to worry and fretting. That's why Isaiah 26:3 is so meaningful for so many people, including myself. Let's look at that verse in several translations.

"The steadfast of mind You will keep in perfect peace, because he trusts in You."

"Thou wilt keep him in perfect peace, whose mind is stayed on thee: because he trusteth in thee" (KJV).

"He will keep in perfect peace all those who trust in him, whose thoughts turn often to the Lord!" (TLB).

"You will guard him and keep him in perfect and constant peace whose mind [both its inclination and its character] is stayed on You, because he commits himself to You, leans on You, and hopes confidently in You" (AMP).

Notice these words: *steadfast, stayed, commits, leans, hopes.* Do you get the sense of those words? It's an ongoing choice. It's a grabbing hold of God and leaning all our weight into Him moment after moment.

Some time ago, I flipped through the doctor's waiting room copy of *National Geographic Magazine* and idly read the Letters to the Editor column. Then one letter caught my eye. Shari Prange of Bonny Doon, California, wrote,

> I enjoyed your article about spiders. One day my husband called me to remove a snake from the carport. "There's no hurry," he said dryly. "It's got a spider web growing on it." Sure enough. I found a motionless baby garter snake eerily coiled and upright like a cobra as the centerpiece of a spider web. But when I went to remove it, I found it was very much alive! It just couldn't pull free from the web. I brushed it off and released it. I'll bet that spider is still dreaming about the big one that got away.[1]

My first reaction was: *Why did her husband call her to remove the snake? Larry never would have called me! I'm afraid of snakes.* But then I saw the spiritual application: Our prayers are as powerful as that spider's web. We can contain our worry through trusting God—by believing He is big enough and powerful enough to handle our problems and concerns.

Other chapters in this book will continue revealing the facts about God and how He is qualified to run our lives. As those truths become more and more real to us we'll be able to first "Pray!" and then "Stay!" We'll stay focused by turning our minds again and again to the Lord, thus wrapping a spider-web-like tenacity and steadfastness about that worry.

I remember a time when my ability to stay was tested. After Larry and I had been married for eighteen months, we decided we wanted to begin a family. I couldn't wait to become a mother. All my life my dream had been to get married and have children. Plus, I hated my job. But we'd decided that I would only quit if I were pregnant. So I was doubly motivated.

But motivation wasn't enough. I couldn't get pregnant. And I was worried . . . very worried! The thought of never becoming a mother was horrifying to me. *God,* I pleaded over and over again, *I just can't imagine that it isn't your will for me to have a child. Please say it's your will! I want a child so badly. What will I do if I can't get pregnant?*

Month after month passed. And then two years had gone by. There were a few false alarms and one time we even whispered to my parents that we thought I was pregnant. We rejoiced together, but it wasn't to be. And I was worried! To the point that I knew the rash that had developed on my hand was because of my worry. I scratched it nervously, wondering if God would withhold this treasured gift from me.

I kept trying to stay focused on trusting God. *Lord, I want to trust you. I want to believe that you know what is best for me. All right, I know you love me. You know what you want to do. I won't worry about it!*

But I didn't have the power to stay in this place of trust. Instead, my mind was like the turning of waves on a storm-tortured sea. Back and forth, back and forth, I gave my worry to God and then took it right back.

Although I never achieved complete trust in God over my worry, God graciously gave me the child I wanted almost five years into our marriage. I was thrilled and humbled that God had mercifully answered my prayer with a yes, even though I hadn't gained total victory over my worry. Later on my failure in this area became an excellent object lesson for me; I sometimes said, "I'm not going to distrust God like I did then." It has been a rainbow-reminder to increase my trust in God when the storm clouds head my way.

Obey! ·····································

Another way to stay tenacious and steadfast is to follow the truth of 2 Corinthians 10:5: "We are destroying speculations and every lofty thing raised up against the knowledge of God, and we are taking every thought captive to the obedience of Christ." The truth of the phrase "we are taking every thought captive to the obedience of

Christ" is most likely the key to my own (sometimes limited) success in gaining victory over worry.

I began to think of worry as an arrow being shot at my mind by Satan. When that happens, I have a choice to either receive it or reject it. I envision grabbing that thought, that worry, that concern, and "taking it captive." In other words, evaluating it and asking myself, "Is this the way God wants me to think?" or "Is this the truth?" Another questioning thought is: "I may be powerless in this situation, but what is God's power?" By these steps I can begin to stay my mind and respond with prayer, not worry. The best way that I can make my mind obey is to claim a Scripture verse.

Let's look at some examples.

Worry	Taking Worry Captive
I love my mother so much, but she's old. How will I cope with her death?	God, you promise not to give me any more than I can handle. I'll enjoy every moment with her now and know that you are in charge of her future. (2 Corinthians 10:13)
My prodigal son could be in big trouble. Maybe he'll end up on the streets and his life in danger. I'm going to try to rescue him.	Lord, I can't really rescue anyone without thwarting your work in their life. I'll believe you will use whatever pain my son has to suffer to draw him to yourself. (Proverbs 19:19)
I may lose my job if I don't make this sale.	Father, give favor for my product to these buyers. You promise to meet all of my true needs, and I believe you will. You are my Provider. (Philippians 4:19)
Our granddaughter has been born prematurely, and her life is in danger. I just couldn't stand it if she dies. What will I do?	Heavenly Father, you know the plans you have for this little girl. Heal her according to your will and give us all the strength to go through whatever you have in mind. (Jeremiah 29:11)

My husband seems distant and uncommunicative. I've got to make him talk to me and get him into counseling.	Lord God, I can't make him do anything. I can only change myself. Give me wisdom in communicating my love and guide me to a counselor for myself. Work in his life and save our marriage. (Philippians 2:3)

Of course there are a thousand scenarios, but the power of taking each worry captive to obey God's Word is powerful. We must stay our minds on the promises of God over and over again.

Here are two ideas for making this "Obey!" principle more meaningful:

Put a rubber band on your wrist. Every time you see that rubber band, let it be a reminder to ask, "Is worry gaining any hold in my mind without my realizing it?" If it is, then snap the rubber band! Give yourself a little pain as motivation to stop worrying.

Create a "peace card." Many years ago I attended a seminar on stress taught by Christian counselor and author Dr. H. Norman Wright. When he talked about worry, he told us to take a 3 x 5 file card and write on one side in big letters, "STOP!" Then on the reverse side we were to write out Philippians 4:6–7. He instructed us, "Every time you begin worrying, pull out your card and say out loud (if possible), 'Stop!' Then turn the card over and repeat the verses."

I began using that card and have recommended that others make their own peace card. In fact, when I speak on worry, I pass out file cards to everyone, and we create them on the spot. I've received a lot of feedback from women, saying how meaningful that was for them.

David Woertendyke has used the truth of 2 Corinthians 10:5 in the past to help him choose to Pray! Stay! and Obey! He shared with me in an e-mail,

> "Worrywart" was a name tag given me as a little boy. Even though it may have seemed merely a sound play on the first five letters of my last name, that frequent labeling really stuck. I became a chronic worrier!

Recently I found that I was lapsing into some old worry habits. Why wouldn't I? I had a perfect invitation—the welfare of my youngest son, who was going through what can only be described as some gruesome times. I awoke at night worrying about him. The spirit of worry may be an infant when we first "adopt" it, but with proper feeding, it will grow. Its pabulum is little worries, and its meat is full-blown, sleep-robbing, stomach-souring worry. When fully grown, it is a monster!

God finally caught my attention when I was whining to a Christian brother about my son's difficult circumstances. In response he simply asked, "Dave, how will your worry make anything better?" Well, that really stunned me. Soon the soul-freeing answer rang loud and clear, "In no way whatsoever!" I felt immediate relief.

Soon, however, I forgot my friend's wisdom and headed back into worry. Then the Holy Spirit whispered quite simply, "Cast down *all* imaginations and bring into captivity *every* thought" (from 2 Corinthians 10:5). I simply repeated His words, and relief, like a wave, came over my soul. It is as though God's wisdom and voice then became my own to minister to my troubled waters. Paul's words continue to offer freedom to my soul.

David learned the power of taking every thought captive to the obedience of Christ as the means to "Obey!" and fight worry.

When it's difficult to trust God with our worries, God graciously responds to our prayers. Like the light reflected into a rainbow, God takes our prayers and reflects them into fulfilling His will for us. That gives us the trust in Him to journey through the rain as we Pray! Stay! Obey!

What storm clouds are you facing? How can you use the rainbow of prayer to solidify your trust in God?

Hannah / 1 SAMUEL 1:1–28

Hannah had a lot to worry about. She desperately wanted a child, and in her culture being barren was regarded as a personal, deprecating comment on a woman's worth and value. Plus, she was harassed by her husband's second, *younger* wife, who made fun of her and "would provoke her bitterly to irritate her" (1 Samuel 1:6). Every year Hannah and her family went to Jerusalem for a feast, and she prayed and prayed. Maybe she felt like this:

"Jehovah, please give me a child. I just can't stand it anymore. I'm so worried that I'll never have a child and I'll have to put up with Peninnah's harassing for the rest of my life. Why have you closed my womb? Don't you love me?"

Hannah continued kneeling and wiping the tears as they streamed down her face. Then an idea seemingly popped into her mind out of nowhere. She muttered to herself, "I'll do anything. . . . I'll even dedicate my son to you to serve in the temple. He'll be yours! And a razor shall never come on his head."

The light touch on her shoulder startled her, and she jumped up from her knees to stand before the priest, Eli. He frowned and said, "Woman, how long will you make yourself drunk? Put away your wine from you."

Horrified that he thought she was a drunkard, Hannah sputtered, "No, my lord, I'm not drunk . . . only sad. I have poured out my soul before God in prayer."

Hannah cringed and then turned her face away, afraid he might even strike her for her audacity. She was surprised to hear him reply gently, "Then go in peace; and may the God of Israel grant your petition that you have asked of Him."

What had he said? Within her a hope as big as a huge rainbow in the sky blossomed. She knew God would grant her desire. "I *will* have a child, I just know it!"

And she did bear a son named Samuel who served in the temple and became a wise leader within Israel. She had several other children after him, and I can only imagine her joy as she walked away that day after hearing Eli's promise from God. She was no longer worried. She was no longer beaten down. She confidently held her head high, knowing God would answer her prayer with a yes. She had prayed; she would stay in the promise of God; and then she obeyed by smiling and eating in faith. We want to be like her, and we can be!

DISCUSSION QUESTIONS

1. What is most meaningful for you about Philippians 4:6?

2. Have you ever felt like, "Hey! Now *this* concern definitely deserves to be worried about!" Explain why that response seemed reasonable at the time and why it became a bit ridiculous (if it did).

3. What do you think about the idea "God helps those who help themselves"? What would you say to someone who gives that as their reason for worrying?

4. Give an example of when you used an "arrow prayer" and when you fought worry with a longer prayer time.

5. If you aren't using a journal, what has been your obstacle to it? Do you want to begin? If so, what steps will you take toward that goal?

6. What do you think about the idea of having a "worry time"? What do you see as advantages and disadvantages? If you plan to use this idea, what time of day will be your "worry time"?

7. Why do you think it's so difficult to remain trusting God about your worry? What have you found effective for keeping your mind focused on God to diminish worry?

8. What worry do you need to "take captive" right now? What truth from Scripture will you use to help you obey?

9. Which tool (the rubber band or the "peace card") will you use today?

10. Whether or not you have experienced a time of infertility, can you relate to Hannah about some prayer that God hasn't answered? How can her example strengthen your faith and trust in God about your own worries?

Letter from God

My Precious Daughter,

I can't wait to hear from you! You are the joy of My heart! I created you to have fellowship with Me, and I love your company when you pray to Me. You are so important to Me that I want you to bring every big and little thing to Me for help, advice, or sharing your joy! I am always available. You'll never find a busy signal, and I don't have a secretary. Prayer is the way you reach Me. Whether it's an arrow prayer or a lengthy one, I welcome it all.

Don't worry if you continue to take back your worries. I am patiently waiting for you to turn them back over to Me again and again. I know that you'll grow stronger each time you focus on Me. I'm confident that My Spirit will continue to work in you to learn this challenging surrender, so don't think I'm upset or unhappy with you. I'll never stop drawing you into My loving embrace.

My daughter, you are valuable and precious to Me. Talk to Me often. Release your worries to Me. I stand ready to respond and take your burdens.

I love you.

Your Heavenly Father

CHAPTER 4

Don't Forget Your *Umbrella*

How Gratitude Protects Your Heart

$\mathcal{I}$t rained in the desert yesterday. We were surprised! It doesn't rain here very often, and even when it does, the clouds most often stay nestled near the mountains. Since we're in the center of the valley, it will often be raining there but not here. One of our fun things to do is to sit out on the patio and watch it rain in the distance. Sometimes there is lightning and thunder, and for a native Californian, that's exciting—we don't have tornado warnings.

That evening, when Larry and I went out to dinner, we left our umbrella in the car. We thought it wasn't raining very hard and decided we didn't really need it, but a cloudburst caught us unawares, and when we walked into the restaurant, we were wet! The umbrella was available, but we unwisely didn't use it.

Just as the umbrella protects us from the rain and keeps us dry, prayer protects us from worry and "stays" our minds to trust in God, resulting in peace. That's what Philippians 4:6–7 promises us: "Be anxious for nothing, but in everything by prayer and supplication with thanksgiving let your requests be made known to God. And the peace of God, which surpasses all comprehension, will guard your hearts and your minds in Christ Jesus."

Peace is what we are all longing for. It's that sigh of relief, the relaxation of the mind, a taking-my-hands-off-because-I-know-God-has-this-in-control kind of feeling. It brings joy, contentment, and tranquility. Isaiah 30:15 says, "For thus the Lord GOD, the Holy One of Israel, has said, 'In repentance and rest you will be saved, in quietness and trust is your strength.' But you were not willing."

OUCH! Quietness is available through trust in God, but when Isaiah gave that message to the people, God said they weren't willing. We want to be willing to have that rest and strength against fear. Philippians 4:7 says peace is the promised result that will "guard" our hearts against worry and fear.

The word *guard* in the Greek is a military term referring to protection by soldiers who surround an area and keep watch. Charles Swindoll calls the word *guard* a "faithful watchdog"[1] and also "a military term for marching sentry duty around something valuable or strategic. When we transfer our troubles to the Lord through prayer, we're given a silent sentry called peace to protect our minds and our emotions."[2]

How can we have the "watchdog" of peace surrounding our hearts, barking at worry and fear? What are the keys to having the umbrella of peace protecting our hearts from Satan's onslaughts? The key is gratitude—having a thankful heart. We'll look at three "A" words that can contribute to gratitude: *appreciation, attention,* and *acclamation.*

Appreciation

The first key for having the umbrella and guard of peace, even when storm clouds close in, is appreciation. Our Philippians verse calls it "thanksgiving." Giving thanks! Focusing on the positive and resisting the temptation to grumble protects our hearts like a soldier standing guard with a gun at his side. In our case, he'll carry an umbrella instead of a gun because we're fighting the storms of life.

We need this guard with his umbrella even more when we are perfectionists. Remember that topic from chapter 2? It's appropriate here also because appreciation can be hard for us perfectionists with our "all or nothing" syndrome. We have a hard time acknowledging something is good if there's a portion of it that is negative. We want to give thanks but we can't seem to take our eyes off the little bit of negative. We lower our umbrella of gratitude and get wet with the "buts. . . ."

Lord, I know I'm supposed to entrust my wayward son to You, *but* how can You work if he isn't listening?

Lord, I know I'm supposed to believe You will provide our rent this month, *but* how can You if I'm not working?

Lord, I know I'm supposed to trust that You are in control of whether or not this breast lump is cancerous, *but* how can breast cancer be for my good?

The list is endless. We might think, *I can't focus on the positive because it's not purely positive. Or, Maybe it's even hypocritical to be positive when there's something negative about the situation.*

A situation doesn't have to be without negatives in order for us to give thanks. That's not being a hypocrite. It's choosing to open the umbrella by trusting God and giving thanks.

My sister, Karen Dye, chose to use the umbrella of gratitude in a worrisome situation. Karen came to Christ because of the stress of a bankrupt business and a house in foreclosure. Later, when Karen and her husband, Stan, moved and opened a pizza restaurant in the small town of Lone Pine, California, she consistently feared the winters because there weren't as many tourists to help their business survive, much less thrive.

She says,

> Finances were always hard. I lived in constant fear of failure and bankruptcy because of the previous loss of our business and home. I felt powerless against it, no matter how hard I worked. When we first moved to Lone Pine and opened Pizza Factory, we were the closest fast food business to the high school. I trusted in the money from the teens to help our finances. But then a hamburger franchise announced they were opening a restaurant nearby. Fear gripped me. I worried, "Oh no, now we're going to go bankrupt for sure!" I secretly hoped that a semi would hit their building or they would burn down. As I whined to God I heard

Him tell me, "I am your hope, not the customers! Bless that other business, don't curse it!"

At first I was shocked but then realized it was true. I needed to put my trust in His sufficiency and stop cursing another business. Romans 12:14 says to bless others and not curse them. So I began making a conscious choice to bless and be grateful for that new hamburger franchise. Every time I thought of it opening and fear gripped my heart, I said out loud, "Lord, bless them! Prosper them!" Of course, at first I didn't say it wholeheartedly, but in time I did. I also didn't have as much fear and worry. The amazing end of the story is that our business did drop that first year the other franchise opened, but we never had trouble paying our bills. At the end of the year I was stunned when I found that even though our sales were down for the year, our net profit was up. In God's economy He had blessed everyone concerned. And the stronghold of worry about my finances broke almost completely. Since then God has financially blessed us beyond our wildest dreams.

Karen opened the umbrella of appreciation through blessing the very thing she worried about.

My writer friend, Joan Clayton, had the same experience. She told me about the time her beloved husband, Emmitt, had been in an automobile accident, and she was called to the hospital. She told me,

> I grabbed my car keys and dashed out the door. All kinds of worries attacked my mind. "Help me, Lord," I cried out. As I pulled into the hospital parking lot, my spirit rose up. The enemy was losing ground. I prayed, "Wait a minute. God, you are my anchor, my rock. Whatever I have to face, you will be with us. You will never leave us. I will walk into that emergency room with confident faith that you are in control and that you bring good out of bad situations. Thank you, Lord. I thank you for your promises and your presence. I feel weak right now, but you are my strength!"
>
> I knew I had to be strong for Emmitt. I walked into the emergency room with boldness. "It's okay, honey. We will be all right!" I exclaimed, giving Emmitt a kiss.
>
> Emmitt breathed a sigh of relief, even though he was strapped to a board with his head in a brace that held him motionless. He

knew I was not falling apart. I felt nothing but peace.

The occupants of the other car had only minor injuries, but Emmitt had broken ribs, whiplash, and atrial fibrillation. The three days we were in the hospital, I thanked God day and night. I could only think of good things. Emmitt's life was spared. We have a new hospital with wonderful doctors and nurses. People had stopped to help Emmitt and had called the ambulance. The policeman was so kind.

After three days and nights I brought Emmitt home, and then the hard part began. He could hardly walk. Since he is six-foot-three and I'm five-foot-four, I had to brace myself to something to help him up. His body was purple all over. The seat belt saved his life but cut him deeply. After two weeks of emotional exhaustion, I lost it one night. I went to bed crying and praying. I was in the twilight zone of half awake and half asleep. "Lord, I feel like a little bird with a broken wing." Immediately I saw in my spirit a beautifully wrapped package in shiny paper. I tore into the package, and there lay a beautiful little bird's wing that sparkled in silver and gold. I fell asleep, slept soundly all night, and arose the next morning completely restored. I just knew this experience had to be in the Bible somewhere, and I found it in Psalms 68:13 (NIV): "Even while you sleep among the campfires, the wings of my dove are sheathed with silver, its feathers with shining gold."

Joan chose to focus on the positives of God's protection and receive His encouragement. She was guarded by her umbrella of thanksgiving. How can you use the umbrella of appreciation to fight worry today?

Attention

The umbrella of gratitude that guards our hearts is harder to open if we don't pay attention to our bodies. The way we treat our bodies can help to build or diminish our peace and our ability to be positive. The Scriptures affirm that it's a lot harder to be grateful during worrisome times of life when our bodies are depleted, malnourished, tired, and stressed. In the book of Proverbs there are several verses that tell it like it is:

Anxiety in the heart of a man weighs it down, but a good word makes it glad. (12:25)

Do not be wise in your own eyes; fear the LORD and turn away from evil. It will be healing to your body and refreshment to your bones. (3:7–8)

A joyful heart is good medicine, but a broken spirit dries up the bones. (17:22)

When our bodies are healthy, we'll find it easier to trust in God with positive thinking. But when we're worried, our bodies can respond with illness and pain or anxiety attacks.

Several years ago I wondered if I was having a mild panic attack when Larry and I traveled to Venezuela, where I was scheduled to speak. After we arrived there, I suddenly had a horrible fear that I would not return home alive. I began to cry and couldn't stop, wondering if I'd ever see our children, Darcy and Mark, again. I knew my fear was ungrounded, but I couldn't stop crying. Larry finally put a guard around me by praying for me and being understanding. I'd never been fearful of flying before, but in that instance worry grabbed hold of me and wouldn't let go. Only the guard of prayer brought me back to reason and trust in God.

Another friend's panic attacks begin whenever her pastor husband shows any kind of concern or care for a woman in his congregation. Even if they are praying for the woman, my friend will suddenly want to run away. Old triggers of abandonment from more than twenty years ago still plague her, and she has gone back into counseling to open the umbrella to protect her heart.

What tools do we have for fighting back when worry assails us?

Professional Christian counseling may be a necessary step for dealing with worry and physical reactions. A wise Christian therapist can help us get to the bottom of something that is triggered by deep-seated fears.

Read books about worry and panic attacks. You might consider *The Anxiety Cure* by Dr. Archibald D. Hart and *The Good News About Worry* by Dr. William Backus.[3]

A good night's sleep is essential to coping with worry. Proverbs 3:24–26 tells us, "When you lie down, you will not be afraid; when you lie down, your sleep will be sweet. Do not be afraid of sudden fear nor of the onslaught of the wicked when it comes; for the LORD will be your confidence and will keep your foot from being caught." When we're exhausted, we are less likely to be able to take hold of the guard of gratitude that God has provided for us. Being tired lessens our ability to stay focused on the Lord. We may need a doctor or therapist's help to come to the point of sleeping well.

Grace told me that when she became Director of Women's Ministries for her church, being in charge of her first retreat was a difficult experience. She was so exhausted that she had a harder time resisting the temptation to compare herself to the former woman in charge, whom everyone adored. She recognized that sleeping so little before the retreat and during it had opened her to Satan's attack of thinking negatively about herself.

When she began thanking God for the difficulties of the retreat and recognized how she could learn from them, she became more grateful for the experience. Then she was able to quit comparing herself to the former director by focusing on the wonderful things God was doing in the retreat.

Exercise is also essential for fighting worry. When I feel the effects of worry begin to nibble at my brain and emotions, I take action. To relieve the tension in my body, I exercise with some sit-up crunches or push-ups (don't be impressed—my knees touch the floor). And my run/walks, sometimes totaling fifteen miles a week, are essential for my physical health and spiritual strength. The endorphins released in the brain during exercise give me a more grateful outlook on life and enable me to commit worrisome problems to God while I'm out watching a beautiful sunrise.

Sabbath rest is a wonderful way to help restore a heart of gratitude, but I find it is one of the most difficult choices for me to make. Since my office is in my home, it's easy to run to my computer to write or work on details, even on Sundays. I've tried over many years, with varying success, to make that day (or another during the week) a time of not working but focusing more on the Lord.

Even yesterday I made that choice and felt more relaxed because of it. Being on a tight deadline for this book, it seemed impossible for me *not* to work on Sunday. But when I had written more on Saturday than I thought possible, the Lord seemed to whisper, "Haven't I given you enough success to last for tomorrow? You thought you'd take two days to accomplish what you did in one. Can you offer Sunday to me as a rest day?"

When I'm successful in surrendering a day to the Lord, it's usually because I remind myself, "God will give me enough time and energy to do what He plans for me."

Finally, *healthy eating* is crucial to having a thankful heart that resists worry. We are influenced spiritually and emotionally by what we eat. And conversely, our spiritual state can sometimes cause good or bad eating habits. For those of us prone to bingeing, my friend Ginny's story is easy to relate to. I know I can relate—just give me the chocolate and no one will get hurt!

She writes,

> I had chocolate chip cookies for dinner last night and for breakfast this morning. The night before last, I had three pieces of pizza for dinner. Think I have issues? My poor choices began after I received a very painful and critical note from a friend. I felt attacked and unfairly accused. I was worried about her opinion of me, and I worried about my own worth and value. Satan worked very hard to get me to believe the old lies—I'm worthless, something's wrong with me, I can't do anything right, God can't possibly love me, etc. I even allowed the lies to lead me to unhealthy actions—the food, for one. I had definitely surrendered to an attitude of ingratitude for who God has made me.
>
> But then I let my husband and a good friend read the note. They both assured me that my feelings were unfounded and that the issues were my friend's, not my own. But oh, Kathy, it's been so painful and it's brought up so many past doubts I believed about myself. Finally this morning I was able to let it go and give it to God. You know how I've been trying to eat more healthfully? Ironically, I did great those two days up until the evening of getting that note. I think I get lonely in the late afternoon and evenings. I'm not sure why. Anyway, I tend to worry more, analyze more, and then struggle more with negative thinking during that time of day. It's such a waste to be good all day and then blow it! I hate that! I'm realizing, though, that there are deeper issues here that I need to deal with.

Ginny shows us that we need to pay attention to those times when we have a harder time focusing on the positive and thanking God for every area of our lives. When we eat healthfully, we'll be strengthened to choose a thankful heart.

Acclamation

A third source of gratitude—that "guard" or umbrella that can protect us from worry—is *acclamation* of the Lord, another word for praise. Acclamation focuses on *who* God is and His attributes. It helps us to resist worry by thanking God for His wonderful nature.

Proverbs 3:5–6 tells us, "Trust in the LORD with all your heart, and do not lean on your own understanding. In all your ways acknowledge Him, and He will make your paths straight." By acknowledging God and seeking Him, we will grow in our ability to be grateful for every aspect of our lives, and not give in to worry.

Here are three ways of doing that:

1. *Rehearse who God is.* One of the primary ways to develop a thankful heart is to study God's nature. I'll be sharing in the next chapter how coming to understand God's sovereignty has done more than anything else to open the umbrella of gratitude to protect me from worry.

But there might be another attribute that speaks more to you. Maybe you'll want to thank Him for His faithfulness—knowing that He is dependable to allow only that which will be for your good and bring Him glory. Or it may be His goodness—that He desires only your good. For some it might be His omnipresence—knowing that He is with you and will stand with you against worry and Satan. There are so many wonderful choices. Truly, you can't go wrong by rehearsing any of God's attributes.

One of the fun ways I like to rehearse His nature is to think of a characteristic of God that starts with each letter of the alphabet. If you're worried, and you're trying to "take every thought captive to the obedience of Christ" (2 Corinthians 10:5), you could think: "God, you are *a*ble, *b*ountiful, *c*aring, *d*etermined to deliver me." Think of those qualities that will give you a grateful heart in the midst of your particular fear. It will help you not to lean on your own understanding, because you are acclaiming Him! Then He'll guide you down a straight path (Proverbs 3:5–6).

Rick Warren writes, "When you think about a problem over and over in your mind, that's called worry. When you think about God's Word over and over in your mind, that's meditation. If you know how to worry, you already know how to meditate! You just need to switch your attention from your problems to Bible verses. The more you meditate on God's Word, the less you will have to worry about."[4] Meditate on God's qualities, and I guarantee that you'll be protected from worry about coming storms or tornados!

2. *Review God's past work.* Can you remember a time when you were worried about something similar to what you're worried about now? Prolific writer Muriel Larson tells this story in an e-mail about having a heart of gratitude in a worrisome situation by reviewing God's past work.

> My husband was out of work, and we were making payments on a new house and car. Then I bumped into a lawyer's car with that new car of ours and he sued us. We were broke and facing payments; I worried myself sick. But then I kneeled by my bed, first thanking God for the ways in which He had helped us in the past. Then I fervently prayed concerning the lawsuit. As I trusted the Lord with my worries, His peace came into my heart. Then a God-given thought came to my mind: "Tomorrow call the lawyer and explain your situation."
>
> I did. The lawyer listened and responded, "When I saw your new car, I didn't realize you were in such a bind. Just send me twenty dollars, and I'll forget the lawsuit." That day I learned two truths that have never failed to help me have peace in every situation. First, I bring everything to the Lord, thanking Him for past answers. Second, I believe He knows the answers to my problems and will guide me by His Spirit.

Like Muriel, you can remember God's intervention from the past. A powerful way to do that is through journaling. Your journal becomes a history book of God's work and how He has revealed His nature through the circumstances of your life. Talk about a faith-building tool that will develop a thankful heart—that's it!

3. *Resist pride and seek humility.* Acclamation of God also puts us in

our place—in the place of humility, that is. When we recognize who God is and who we are not, we're grateful that we don't have to worry about taking God's place in other people's lives and circumstances. We don't have to feel responsible for providing what God wants to provide.

And we can also be grateful that God is in charge of taking care of our reputation. Worry can rear its ugly head when I'm worried about what other people think of me. I can't be the only one who is careful about her reputation, can I? Be assured that I'm not talking about an "I'm a worm" kind of humility. Don't think of *yourself* that way, because I won't allow you to refer to someone I care about like that!

Instead, we need to have the attitude that Romans 12:3 talks about: "For through the grace given to me I say to every one among you not to think more highly of himself than he ought to think; but to think so as to have sound judgment, as God has allotted to each a measure of faith." That's a realistic view of us. You are truly valuable and important, God's creation who is useful for His purposes. God wants us to be grateful for who He has made us to be!

If we have this positive perspective, we won't be worried and fearful about how someone else views us. We'll trust God with

- materialism: we don't have to keep up with the Joneses;
- gossip: we don't have to clear our own names or defend ourselves;
- ministry success: the results belong to God, not us;
- our children's behavior: we recognize that they are reflections of themselves, not us.

Think of the worry you are facing today. Which of the three ways to acclaim God would you like to focus on today so that you can be protected by a thankful heart? Will you rehearse who God is? Review God's past work? Resist pride and seek humility? If you will use at least one of these tools, you'll find the umbrella of gratitude shielding you from worry. You can guard your heart so that worry doesn't create a lack of gratefulness and worship and wipe out your trust in God. Make a new commitment that you will use the umbrella of *appreciation, attention,* and *acclamation.*

Michal / 1 SAMUEL 18:20–19:24;
2 SAMUEL 6:16–23

Michal had a lot to worry about. In fact, she was most worried about what others thought of her. The wife of David in the Old Testament, Michal sadly let her own reputation and her need for prestige get in the way of her marriage and her commitment to God. Michal started out as David's first wife and deeply loved him. But difficult circumstances (being taken away from David and given to another man as his wife) forced their way upon her, and as a result Michal's heart grew cold.

After nine years or more (we're not sure exactly how long) Michal is returned to King David, but by now he has other wives and many children. What a dirty trick. But the prestige of being the queen still seemed to hold considerable attraction for her.

Unfortunately, by the time Michal is returned to David, both her heart and his have changed and their former devotion to each other is no longer there. Too much water has passed under the bridge.

Michal may have felt insecure in her position, and with the other wives lurking about, she may have felt threatened and jealous. Michal didn't guard her heart with a spirit of gratitude for the position God had restored to her, and worry may have kicked open the door.

Then came the defining moment, when her unguarded heart allowed worry to overwhelm her. Instead of being grateful for her position, she reacted. And it wasn't a pretty sight. When David accompanied the return of the ark to Jerusalem with dancing, out of his passion for God, Michal despised him. When he returned home, she criticized him; she wasn't grateful for his heart toward God.

She may have had a worried heart and reacted to him out of fear and concern. Maybe as she viewed David dancing from that window, she was thinking, *O Lord, look at that man! What are the neighbors thinking? Unclothed and uncouth! That's a sight only I should be viewing! We shouldn't be mingling with the common people like this! It is just so embarrassing! There goes* my *reputation in the neighborhood!*

How sad. The biblical account says that David spurned Michal from then on and she never had children. In other words, she lived alone and lonely.

Michal's heart was not guarded. Yes, she experienced terrible, unfair things in her life. But she could have chosen to give thanks and praise God along with David. Instead, she allowed pride, prestige, and power to cloud her thinking and ultimately ruin her life.

We don't want to be like Michal, and we don't have to be.

 ## DISCUSSION QUESTIONS

1. When peace rules in your heart and mind, what does it feel like? When you read Philippians 4:7 and Isaiah 30:15, what do you think the words *peace* and *quietness* mean?

2. Can you think of any other descriptions that are similar to the words *watchdog, guard,* or *umbrella*?

3. Do you find it easy or difficult to be appreciative? In other words, do you see the glass as half empty or half full? How do you think your family and friends would characterize you? If there's a discrepancy between how they perceive you and how you perceive yourself, why do you think that's so?

4. Can you think of a time that "all or nothing" thinking prevented you from expressing gratitude and appreciation?

5. Of the three verses from Proverbs (12:25; 3:7–8; 17:22), which is most meaningful to you? How does each speak to you?

6. If you have experienced panic attacks, describe what it feels like. How has God helped you to cope?

7. Of the physical needs we all have (sleep, exercise, rest, healthy eating), which one do you feel you need to work on improving?

8. If needed, how could professional Christian counseling or reading other books about worry and/or panic attacks help you?

9. For each of the three ways for acclaiming God, give an example of how you've trusted God by rehearsing who God is; reviewing God's past work; resisting pride and seeking humility.

10. How do you see pride fueling worry in your life? How can the truth of Romans 12:3 help combat that?

11. Scan through Michal's story in 1 Samuel 14:49; 1 Samuel 18–19; 1 Samuel 25:44; 2 Samuel 3:13–14; 2 Samuel 6:16–23. How would you describe her story overall? In what ways did she neglect guarding her heart from worry and negativity? What do you learn from her story?

12. From this chapter, what one thing do you want to concentrate on as your umbrella of protection against the storms of worry?

Letter from God

My Precious Daughter,

You can be protected! I've designed you to be protected through the way your mind works. Gratitude is one of the most powerful ways to shield your heart and mind from worry. For when you choose to be grateful, you are focusing on My goodness in your life. Even when things aren't perfect, give thanks anyway—it'll help you to concentrate on the positive and trust Me for the negative. I'm sure you've noticed that little in your world is purely one way. But guess what? My love and concern for you is totally "one way"! It's never watered down. I love you too much for that!

So choose to appreciate even the smallest positive things. Choose to praise Me! I want you to praise Me because it's good for you. Soon, instead of turning to worry in an attempt to control the problems in your life, you will learn to trust Me by praising Me. You will begin to feel relieved, renewed, and refreshed because your trust in Me will grow as you recognize My qualities. I want you to know Me so that you will develop a grateful heart.

Remember that your body is not capable of withstanding unlimited stress and worry. I want you to need Me! Cooperate with Me by caring for your body. Then you'll be able to cast your cares upon Me even more!

Daughter, are you convinced yet of My great love for you? I hope so. But whether you are or not, I'll keep telling you.

I love you.

Your Heavenly Father

CHAPTER 5

Seeing Past
the Snowstorm

How God's Sovereignty Provides

I was speaking at a Christian women's meeting at a country club in the mountains on the subject of worry, and I was worried! As I looked out the huge glass windows of the restaurant at the beautiful tree-filled mountain, I saw the snow start to fall. Even as I talked, I thought, *I'm supposed to drive home today so that I can leave for another speaking engagement tomorrow. I've got to get off this mountain. Driving in snow is scary!*

I finished my talk and enjoyed visiting with the women at my book table, but at the back of my mind, I was thinking, *Oh no, the snow is still coming down! I've got to get out of here before I get snowed in.*

A few minutes later, after packing my materials and books into the car, I slowly drove out of the parking lot. And then I felt it—my car began fishtailing in the snow. *Oh no, I don't have much experience driving in the snow. I'm scared!* was my first reaction.

But then the thought hit me: *Wait a minute! I have four-wheel drive on this SUV. Why didn't I think of that before? I'm safe!*

I switched gears, and the tires immediately grabbed hold of the road. Whew! I let out my caught breath and breathed easier. *Okay, I'm going to be fine. I'm safe! I'm on my way.*

That day I experienced the security of depending upon my four-wheel drive to keep me safe, and I was able to get down the mountain without any difficulties. The four-wheel drive that I depended upon on that mountain is like God's sovereignty in our battle against worry.

The fact that God is totally and mightily in control of our lives and this whole universe gives us a security much like our tires grabbing onto the road. Without the four-wheel drive, we might be skidding around, and without an awareness and dependence upon God's sovereignty to provide everything we truly need, worry can have the same effect—create havoc and insecurity in our lives. What a difference when we look at life through the filter of God's sovereignty. No matter how the snowstorms rage around us, we are safe and sound.

As I mentioned in a previous chapter, I began studying God's attributes many years ago, and since then my favorite characteristic of God has been His sovereignty. It's a wonderful part of God's nature and gives us such peace and confidence when things seem to be out of control.

God is not wringing His hands, wondering what He's going to do to help us in our troubles. He hasn't been caught unawares by our struggles. He's not overwhelmed with our earthly problems and fears. Instead, He knows the plan that He has for each potential trouble. Understanding and meditating on His sovereignty will give us tremendous peace in a worrisome world.

But what is sovereignty? Charles Swindoll defines it this way: "Our all-wise, all-knowing God reigns in realms beyond our comprehension to bring about a plan beyond our ability to alter, hinder, or stop."[1] I love that definition because it reminds us that God is God and we are not!

Maybe you are wondering, "But what about our will, our God-given ability to choose? Hasn't He told us that we are responsible for the choices we make? How then can He also be totally in control?"

What you're saying is true, and I'm not exactly sure how those two seeming contradictions work together. I haven't even found theologians who can explain the paradox. But I do know that God is totally sovereign while you and I have the ability to make decisions.

Somehow they dovetail together, and God's hands are not bound by our decisions. Knowing God is sovereignly in control and in charge of my world gives me incredible peace and confidence. So I don't have to worry, even when the snowstorms of life hit.

Let's look at a passage of Scripture that will help us strengthen this belief. It's Matthew 6:25–33:

> For this reason I say to you, do not be worried about your life, as to what you will eat or what you will drink; nor for your body, as to what you will put on. Is not life more than food, and the body more than clothing? Look at the birds of the air, that they do not sow, nor reap nor gather into barns, and yet your heavenly Father feeds them. Are you not worth much more than they? And who of you by being worried can add a single hour to his life? And why are you worried about clothing? Observe how the lilies of the field grow; they do not toil nor do they spin, yet I say to you that not even Solomon in all his glory clothed himself like one of these. But if God so clothes the grass of the field, which is alive today and tomorrow is thrown into the furnace, will He not much more clothe you? You of little faith! Do not worry then, saying, "What will we eat?" or "What will we drink?" or "What will we wear for clothing?" For the Gentiles eagerly seek all these things; for your heavenly Father knows that you need all these things. But seek first His kingdom and His righteousness; and all these things will be added to you. So do not worry about tomorrow; for tomorrow will care for itself. Each day has enough trouble of its own.

Let's look at each verse and see what we can find to help us gain victory over worry.

It's All About God, Not About You!

"For this reason I say to you, do not be worried about your life, as to what you will eat or what you will drink; nor for your body, as to what you will put on. Is not life more than food, and the body more than clothing?" (v. 25).

We get confused sometimes and worry about the unimportant. Jesus says that our needs aren't the most significant thing. The snowflakes of worry can obscure our vision, making us unable to see God's important role in our lives. It's our relationship—our life—with Him that is significant, not our clothing or food. Jesus is not saying we shouldn't take responsibility for our lives or that we should be careless about the future. But He doesn't want us to be worried, anxious, or distracted by the very needs that God has *every* intention of meeting.

Notice the emphasis in that verse upon *my* own needs. He addresses those who are selfishly thinking only about themselves: "What shall *we* eat?" or "What shall *we* drink?" and "What are *we* going to wear?" Worry does that to us! It creates insecurity in God's ability to provide, and then we focus on ourselves. It creates an argumentative spirit within us that says, "What about *me*? It's all about *me*!"

That was our daughter Darcy's attitude when she was a teenager, arguing with us about our decisions. A strong-willed girl, she could out-debate anyone. We kept telling her, "Please grow up and be an attorney. You'll be able to take care of us in our old age!" In the meantime, however, I was frantic as I tried to convince her I was the mother and she was not!

One day I heard of a wonderful retort for Darcy's persistent questioning. From then on I became a "broken record." If Darcy was merely arguing for the sake of argument rather than looking for truth, I calmly said, "Regardless of your argument, do what I said." I kept saying that even though she continued to argue. In time she realized that her questioning wasn't working and she replied, "Don't say 'regardless'!" Then I said, "*Nevertheless*, do what I said!"

I wonder if that is God's response to us when we ask, "What will *we* eat? What will *we* drink? What will *we* wear?"

He's saying, "Regardless, I will provide for you. I'm God! You're not! Let me sovereignly take care of you."

You may not have a sense that you are arguing with God, but that may be what you are doing when you ask, "Are you going to take care of me, God?"

It's All About Him, Not About You . . . But You Are Important!

Even though this passage in Matthew is all about God and His sovereign provision for His own, Jesus goes on to stress how important each of us is to Him. He says, "Look at the birds of the air, that they do not sow, nor reap nor gather into barns, and yet your heavenly Father feeds them. Are you not worth much more than they?" (v. 26).

When we consider the fact that God isn't wringing His hands in worry, we wonder why we worry at all. Jerry Bridges, in his book *The Practice of Godliness*, writes,

> So why do we worry? Because we do not believe. We are not really convinced that the same Jesus who can keep a sparrow in the air knows where our lost luggage is, or how we are going to pay that auto repair bill, or how we can get to our destination on time. Or if we believe that He can deliver us through our difficulties, we doubt if He will. We let Satan sow seeds of doubt in our minds about His love and care of us.[2]

God loves us so much that He doesn't want to add low self-esteem to our worry. Jesus assures us that we are very important, even more important than the birds He graciously provides for. He shows His sovereign care by making sure each of His creatures gets all they need. Yes, there is horrible famine, genocide, and poverty in this world, and terrible things happen even to believers, but I've heard stories from imprisoned believers in third world countries of God providing for all their *true* needs. They could rejoice in His supernatural care—even without the luxury and "things" that we Americans think we can't live without.

On the basis of verses like Psalm 37:25 ("I have been young, and now I am old, yet I have not seen the righteous forsaken or his descendants begging bread") and Philippians 4:19 ("And my God will supply all your needs according to His riches in glory of Christ Jesus"), we know that those who believe and trust in Him will be taken care of—even in the midst of a snowstorm of problems and danger!

Mary Whitson Langley, a freelance writer, gave me an interesting perspective of this. She wrote me,

> My husband used to call me a worrywart. I worried about everything. I often gave God my cares, but I would take them back by constantly nagging God with my worries. I knew that if one truly believed God's promises, there would be no need for the nagging or worrying, but it was hard to do.

Then my husband died a few years ago. Being a twin, I had never been alone, even before I was born. I worried constantly, especially at night. I was lonely and afraid. Then one day I noticed one of those little surveillance cameras you see everywhere. My fears turned to real faith in my heavenly Father. I realized God sovereignly watches over me like a camera. Luke 12:6–7 tells us, "Are not five sparrows sold for two farthings, and not one of them is forgotten before God? But even the very hairs of your head are all numbered. Fear not therefore: ye are of more value than many sparrows" (KJV). It is a comfort to know we are always under the surveillance of God's watchful eye.

God does watch over us and wants to provide for all of our needs. Of course, for us humans, the problem is that little word *need*. Philippians 4:19 assures us, "And my God shall supply all your *wants* according to His riches in glory in Christ Jesus" (Kathy's version).

You see, God is telling us . . .

What? You're saying that verse isn't correct?

But that's the way I *want* it to read. God will supply all my *wants* . . .

Oh, all right, you're correct. That verse doesn't read that way; it actually says, "God shall supply all your *needs* . . ." Big difference, isn't it? I would prefer that He gave me all my wants, but that's not what is really necessary. Yet God is so generous that He often provides my needs *and* my wants. Because He's in total charge of the universe, He can do that easily, with no great effort.

By the way, maybe that's why we have a hard time trusting God for our needs or wants. We're afraid it's too much effort for Him. We think He's lost in the snowstorm just like we would be. But let's be assured that whether He's providing for the birds of the air or for our needs, both are equally easy for Him. It's as simple as calling it into existence, like He did the whole universe. No big deal! He's that big of a God.

My friend and fellow speaker Pam Farrel (coauthor of the book *Men Are Like Waffles, Women Are Like Spaghetti*) told me the following story of how God sovereignly provided the care she needed.

She had been traveling with back-to-back speaking engagements and was exhausted. She looked forward to getting to her destination early so that she could take a nap. But when she arrived at the Denver airport, she was disappointed to learn her connecting flight had been cancelled. She would have to endure five hours in the airport—instead of relaxing in a hotel room. She worried about not being rested for her next speaking engagement, and cried out to God, "This sure isn't taking care of me! I'm exhausted. Show me what to do, because I'm so tired I can barely think."

As she walked and prayed she spotted an empty gate with a difference—this one had a door to the outside, which was propped open, letting in fresh air! She felt the Holy Spirit whisper, *"There!"* Pam created her own lounge chair with her suitcase under her legs and her purse under her head. She began reading, but she was distracted when some birds hopped into the terminal and began to feed on crumbs. Again God's Spirit whispered, *"Pam, remember how I take care of the birds? You're more valuable than they are!"* Pam remembered Matthew 6:26 and heard God continue, *"I will take care of you!"*

Within a few moments she drifted off to a sweet slumber—in the airport! When she awoke an hour later she felt completely rested and refreshed, ready to handle whatever else God allowed on her trip.

God is in control. He can do anything He wants! He can provide sweet slumber in an airport or in a high-priced hotel. And we don't have to get upset worrying about whether or not or *how* He's going to do it. Joyce Meyer writes, "In verse 25, Jesus commands us to look at the birds of the air. Have you ever seen a bird in a tree having a nervous breakdown? Just as God feeds the birds and animals and even clothes the grass and flowers of the field, so He will feed and clothe those of us who put our faith and trust in Him."[3]

It's All About God; It's Not About Your Stature!

Anxiety, worry, fretting, or any of its variations don't do a single bit of good! The whiteout of a snowstorm clouds our spiritual vision, keeping us from believing that God is in charge and can do anything He wants. That's why Jesus continues by saying, "Who of you by worrying can add a single hour to his life?" (Matthew 6:27 NIV).

Rick Joyner says, "God answers prayers, not worry."[4] You will have more success adding to your life's span with prayer than you will with worry. Worry doesn't reach the sovereign God of the universe. But He is all ears on His throne when prayers reach Him.

Since commentators say that adding "a single cubit to his life's span" (v. 27) refers to both the length of life and our physical stature, this verse is for all of us who don't like the shape we're in, or the nose we have, or the color of our hair, or . . . whatever. All of us have something in our physical appearance that bothers us.

But Psalm 139:13–15 assures us, "For You formed my inward parts; You wove me in my mother's womb. I will give thanks to You, for I am fearfully and wonderfully made; wonderful are Your works, and my soul knows it very well. My frame was not hidden from You, when I was made in secret, and skillfully wrought in the depths of the earth."

God's sovereignty extends to every area of your life. You were created *exactly* the way He wanted you to be for His purposes. Over the years I've struggled to trust God's sovereignty because of what I judged to be a big nose and small breasts. And in my childhood I hated that I was tall. But now those things are insignificant (and no longer sources of worry) because I know my true value and importance are not dependent upon those physical features.

Shirley Shibley learned that this principle applied to the growth of her children. She wrote to me,

> When my children were infants I walked with fear at my side. Were they developing as they should? Was I a proper mother? I worried about the soon-to-come "terrible twos." When I weathered that age, I worried that my toddlers would not be adequately prepared for school. When they were school-age, I was afraid they would get into trouble or fail a grade. And adolescence? I'd seen some children's personalities change abruptly from sweet to ugly at that age, and I lay awake worrying every time I saw the slightest indication my children were rebelling.
>
> Then I finally realized that I had wonderful children and God had been caring for them all along! They grew because of difficult times and mistakes. Worry robbed me of simply enjoying my children at each stage. Now as grown adults, my children are still learning to trust God more and more each day. That is what their mother—me!—is finally learning to do also.

Are you learning that too? If you struggle with anxiety about wanting to "add a single cubit" to your stature or that of anyone else, make a choice to say, "God, I am going to trust your sovereignty. You could have made me any way you wanted, and you desired this for me. I choose to trust you and thank you" (and if you need to, you can add), "even though I'm not completely sure. . . ." By making that decision, even with some reservations, you may be able to cross that worry off your list!

It's All About God; It's Not About Clothing!

Jesus continues in Matthew 6 by addressing what we gals are often concerned about: clothes! Jesus really does cover all the bases, doesn't He? After all, when the snowstorm hits, we must be warmly dressed. So let's see what He has in mind.

> "And why are you worried about clothing? Observe how the lilies of the field grow; they do not toil nor do they spin, yet I say to you that not even Solomon in all his glory clothed himself like one of these. But if God so clothes the grass of the field, which is alive today and tomorrow is thrown into the furnace, will He not much more clothe you? You of little faith! Do not worry then, saying, 'What will we eat?' or 'What will we drink?' or 'What will we wear for clothing?'" (vv. 28–31).

I believe Jesus' list is a representation of *all* our needs. He isn't limiting His remarks only to clothes (or food in the previous verses), but is saying, "If God will provide these needs, then He'll provide *every* need." That's why I also love 1 Chronicles 29:11–12: "Yours, O LORD, is the greatness and the power and the glory and the victory and the majesty, indeed everything that is in the heavens and the earth; Yours is the dominion, O LORD, and You exalt Yourself as head over all. Both riches and honor come from You, and You rule over all, and in Your hand is power and might; and it lies in Your hand to make great and to strengthen everyone."

Concerned about your finances? God is sovereign over that. Concerned about getting the promotion you need? God is sovereign over that. Concerned about getting the admiration you need? God is sovereign over that. Concerned about strength to do what God has called you to do? God is sovereign over that too.

And guess what? The best part is that Jesus *wants* you to feel important, valued, and worthwhile! Not just wants; He longs, yearns, even craves for you to know the significance He places upon you. Because you are His cherished creation, He's going to meet all your needs.

Dana Finch discovered that recently. She has spoken for many years in the secular business arena and then felt God was guiding her into speaking for the Christian community. She didn't know how to make it happen, but she had been preparing for God's provision by setting up her Web site, logo, and brochure.

She told me,

> God confirmed His sovereign touch upon it all last Monday when I was teaching a business workshop, and a friend I know from a neighboring town attended. We went to lunch and I shared what the Lord has been doing. She began to smile, so I asked her what she was smiling about. She answered, "Dana, I heard you speak last year and immediately began praying for you because I knew you should be teaching Christian women. I want you to be our speaker for our church women's retreat next fall."
>
> WOW! God reminded me that it is in His sovereign timing and leading that He will give me opportunities. It was a humbling reminder that I don't need to worry.

Does God want you to have that job you're seeking? Then He'll sovereignly give you favor with the boss. Does God want you to have new furniture? Then He can supply a good price. Does God want you to be on that committee? Then He will provide the invitation. Whatever He wants for you, He will sovereignly provide for you.

But that doesn't mean that we never take action. His sovereignty doesn't represent a fatalistic kind of perspective that takes away any involvement or decision-making on our part. We are expected to cooperate with God as we follow His leading in each of the situations outlined above. The important thing isn't whether or not we have a big or small part in what God brings into our lives. What I want to emphasize here is that all of our worrying *does not* contribute anything positive to our lives. We can trust God to bring things to pass as we respond to His leading in every circumstance of life.

It's All About God; Not About Tomorrow!

Jesus continues teaching, wrapping up His sermon on sovereignty: "'For the Gentiles eagerly seek all these things; for your heavenly Father knows that you need all these things. But seek first His kingdom and His righteousness, and all these things will be added to you. So do not worry about tomorrow; for tomorrow will care for itself. Each day has enough trouble of its own'" (Matthew 6:32–34).

I'm worried! I've been wondering, *If I get breast cancer, should I take traditional chemotherapy or try a nutritional approach?*

No, I don't have breast cancer, but I was just wondering what I should do if I get it. You see, several of my friends and acquaintances have breast cancer, and I was just hoping to plan now what I should do.

I hope you're laughing, because I am! Although I wasn't laughing when the snowflakes of worry made me mull over those ideas for several days. Those thoughts are how the "Gentiles" think. Jesus is pointing out that they don't trust God. They "buy" trouble in case they need to cash it in later.

We don't want to be like that! Jesus is telling us that tomorrow is in God's hands, and we're supposed to be concentrating on today, not worrying about tomorrow. When I'm worrying about what kind of therapy I'll take if I get breast cancer tomorrow, what is my view of today? It's muddied and sullied by worry.

God will take care of tomorrow. Yes, I should make plans *for whatever I truly have control over in the future*. But not for those things over which I have *no control*. If I seek His kingdom, if I obey what He wants me to do today and follow His promptings for any planning for tomorrow, then I can entrust tomorrow to God.

Herman, unfortunately, couldn't quite trust in that. Yesterday Larry and I had lunch at our friends John and Dixie Murray's home, and they told us about their cat, Herman. Herman has gone to cat heaven now, but we were enthralled to hear about him.

Herman was a twenty-pound, black and white mixed cat who loved to eat. And John and Dixie were generous in feeding him. But when the food in Herman's bowl got a little thin—you know, he could see the bottom through some of the food?—he got nervous. He would pace and meow and look up at John and Dixie, worried that his bowl wasn't *full* of food. John and Dixie laughed when they saw the pacing, meowing, and worry-lines on Herman's forehead. After all, the bowl wasn't even empty yet; we're talking "starting to see a tiny portion of the bottom of his bowl while there's still plenty of food."

As John and Dixie pointed out to us, within a foot of Herman's bowl was a pantry with a ten-pound bag of cat food. There was always plenty, but Herman couldn't trust in that; if the bowl started to look empty, he figured there was something to worry about!

Worry is unnecessary for us too. We are more important than Herman, the birds of the air, or the flowers in the field. When you feel like you're beginning to fishtail on the snowy road, remember to switch to four-wheel drive. Trust in God's sovereignty to provide for every need you have. He knows what's best and He will do it. It's not about you; it's all about God!

Naomi / Book of RUTH

Naomi had *a lot* to worry about! After her husband and both of her sons died in a foreign land, Naomi trudged back to her native land with one of her son's widows, Ruth. When she returned to her home in Bethlehem hardly anyone recognized her, so great was her grief and depression. When she identified herself, she explained, "Do not call me Naomi; call me Mara, for the Almighty has dealt very bitterly with me. I went out full, but the LORD has brought me back empty. Why do you call me Naomi, since the LORD has witnessed against me and the Almighty has afflicted me?" (Ruth 1:20–21).

Naomi was correct in identifying God's hand upon her. She recognized His sovereignty, but she didn't trust Him. She couldn't look at her trials and tribulations, thinking, *It's all about God!* All she could think was, *It's all about me! And it isn't pretty. Look what God has done to me.*

God had every intention of providing for her, but in her gloomy outlook of focusing only on the difficulties, clouded by the snowstorm of deep grief, she allowed her trust to be overcast by worry. The forecast certainly didn't look sunny. Only snow and rain were predicted in her future.

However, in the end, Naomi did recognize God's provision. Her daughter-in-law, Ruth, married a rich relative named Boaz, and soon Naomi was blessed with a grandson.

Her story finishes with this forecast of hope:

> Then the women said to Naomi, "Blessed is the LORD who has not left you without a redeemer today, and may his name become famous in Israel. May he also be to you a restorer of life and a sustainer of your old age; for your daughter-in-law, who loves you and is better to you than seven sons, has given birth to him." Then Naomi took the child and laid him in her lap, and became his nurse. The neighbor women gave him a name, saying, "A son has been born to Naomi!" So they named him Obed. He is the father of Jesse, the father of David. (Ruth 4:14–17)

Naomi's story shows us both God's sovereignty and His faithfulness. He didn't give up on Naomi, even though she was defeated and blind to His love for her. Naomi turned back to the Lord. In that, we want to be just like her, and we can be!

 DISCUSSION QUESTIONS

1. If you have studied God's nature, what is your favorite attribute of God?

2. What speaks to your heart the most when you read Charles Swindoll's definition of God's sovereignty ("Our all-wise, all-knowing God reigns in realms beyond our comprehension to bring about a plan beyond our ability to alter, hinder, or stop.")?

3. Have you found a way to solve the paradox of God's sovereignty alongside the God-given ability of men to make their own choices? If so, how do you explain it?

4. Look again at Matthew 6:25. In what way have you said the same thing? Have you ever thought of it as arguing with God? How

does that make your comments to God seem?

5. Do you find the analogy about your being more important than birds effective in persuading your heart to trust in God? If not, why not? If so, why?

6. How does Philippians 4:19 increase your trust in God?

7. In what way have you felt discontented or worried about your physical appearance or frame? How do Matthew 6:27 and Psalm 139:13–15 help you fight against this worry? Can you identify some ways that God has used the thing you dislike about yourself?

8. Which of the needs expressed in Matthew 6:25–31 is your greatest worry? How do Matthew 6:28–32 and 1 Chronicles 29:11–12 minister to you?

9. What worry about the future bothers you right now? Jesus is saying to you, "Therefore do not be worried about _____ (write in your worry)." Does hearing Jesus talk to you about it help you?

10. How does your body react when you "borrow" worries from tomorrow? How has your vision experienced a snow whiteout today?

11. Scan the biblical book of Ruth. In what ways are you like Naomi? How does God's provision for her increase your trust in Him?

Letter from God

My Precious Daughter,

    You are more important to Me than birds, flowers, nature . . .

everything! *Anything else that I created is far less important than you are! You are the crowning touch of My creation. I had you in mind from the very beginning, and I have the capability of loving each of my human creations equally and with as much passion as I love everyone else. You are my unique conception; I designed you exactly the way I envisioned from the beginning. Nothing is a mistake. I don't ever make junk!*

Please don't think poorly of yourself for any reason. Even your sin is covered by My Son's blood. I want you to see yourself the way I see you: important, valuable, and worth what My Son did for you. You are the apple of My eye, and My love for you never wavers, fluctuates, or dips. It is consistent and dependable. Won't you absorb it all?

Precious woman of God, I promise to provide for all your true needs. Have you noticed My generosity? I also want to thrill you with things that you want sometimes. I love to see you rejoicing in Me. It's my desire that you love Me not only because of what I give you but also because you have come to know My heart. Trust Me. Don't worry. I'll supply for you because you are of inestimable value to Me.

I love you.

Your Heavenly Father

CHAPTER 6

April Showers Bring *May Flowers*

Seeing the Purpose in Troubles

 $\mathcal{I}$ n chapter 4 I mentioned how surprised I was to see rain in the desert. Well, because of that rain, we are having the most marvelous profusion of flowers. The verbena are growing and blooming everywhere, especially in vacant lots. Their purple flowers are appearing even in places I've never seen them before. And soon the ocotillo will bloom. That's a tall plant that normally looks like sticks jutting out of the ground. But after it rains they get inspired with round leaves up and down each "stick" and orange flowers at the top. I never would have thought the desert could have so many wild flowers, but it has proved itself worthy of the rain it received. The rain brought an unexpected benefit, and we are enjoying it.

Maybe you've thought, *If I could just see some reason for what I fear, maybe then I wouldn't be so worried!* Just like that rain brought flowers and greenery, the potential trials and tribulations that we worry about will also bring benefits and advantages—if they actually happen!

As we discussed in chapter 1, God's Word promises that even if what we fear happens, God promises to bring something good from it. In this chapter, we'll examine more closely what our attitudes should be about potential problems and how we should handle them.

Don't Be Surprised!

Sometimes worry catches us off guard because we're surprised we're having problems. Our worry is based in thoughts like, *I don't deserve problems! If I'm having them, I must have something to worry about!* Kari West, who experienced a divorce, expresses it this way,

> When your expectations about life and love are shattered, you get over building castles in the air. You discover there is no such place as an idyllic abode. You catch sight of how loss is moving you past your personal standards to what God expects of you. You start seeing how your expectations got in the way of reality, leading to disappointment. You begin to notice how the unrealistic and the unrealized distract you from what really matters. You see how much of your disappointment is because life, God, or somebody else failed to fulfill or live up to your expectations.
>
> It has taken years, but I'm finally getting the picture. I expected more than this life could ever deliver. In the cold glare of reality, I now realize that life in this fallen world is not and has never been fair. It will never be a warm-fuzzy painting. *Life is what it is.*[1]

Kari is echoing what 1 Peter 4:12–13 tells us: "Beloved, do not be surprised at the fiery ordeal among you, which comes upon you for your testing, as though some strange thing were happening to you; but to the degree that you share the sufferings of Christ, keep on rejoicing, so that also at the revelation of His glory you may rejoice with exultation."

Some commentators believe that Peter may have been referring to the "fiery ordeal" that some Christians experienced during that time period. Since Christians had been blamed for the burning of Rome during Nero's time, Peter, along with other Christians, may have feared that officials might follow their emperor's example and burn them at the stake. Not a pretty thought! Certainly something to be worried about, right?

NOT! Peter says this isn't something strange or unusual. Trials are to be expected, and worry is not a godly response. Instead, we are commanded to rejoice! The word for "rejoice" could also be translated, "overjoyed"! Overjoyed about being burned at the stake? You've got to be kidding! Peter says, yes, even rejoice about that, because trials bring glory.

I like the words for "surprise" that the Amplified Bible uses. That version says, "Beloved, do not be amazed and bewildered at the fiery ordeal which is taking place to test your quality, as though something strange (unusual and alien to you and your position) were befalling you" (v. 12). Amazed? Bewildered? Yes, I've felt those emotions.

The Message reads, "Friends, when life gets really difficult, don't jump to the conclusion that God isn't on the job. Instead, be glad that you are in the very thick of what Christ experienced. This is a spiritual refining process, with glory just around the corner."

We may fear that God isn't on the job, but don't be alarmed. He hasn't left His post. In fact, I like to remember that all (every single one) of our problems are required to go through God's love filter. When I share this concept at speaking engagements, I hold up a cheesecloth and ask, "What is a cheesecloth used for?" Everyone answers, "Filtering and straining food." Of course! Then I wrap that cheesecloth around me and explain, "This cheesecloth represents God's love filter. Nothing can pass through His love filter except what He desires to use for our good and His glory. Nothing!"

If we're worried and surprised about a particular problem or difficulty reaching us, then we're saying in effect, "God has a hole in His love filter! He doesn't really love me or want the best for me. He must not be keeping His 'cheesecloth' repaired." But there are no holes in God's love filter; it is completely intact, and He lovingly filters out whatever should not reach us.

Now, this doesn't mean we should never take action about a difficulty. Worry results from our being passive when God is saying, "Do what I tell you!" For instance, when a wife is being abused by her husband, God wants her to take action to protect herself! Yes, this problem has gone through God's love filter, but that doesn't mean she should allow it to continue. We shouldn't be surprised at trials because very often God is saying, "Do something about it!"

Not only should we not be surprised at the trials that can worry us, we also shouldn't be surprised that we have anxiety and tension in our lives. Christian psychologist Dr. William Backus writes,

> Many people . . . hate to be reminded of reality. They . . . try to convince themselves that they must be able to get through life without pain if only they have enough "faith" (which they take to mean something like a high-decibel "spirituality"). Some people even take it to mean they're shoddy Christians if they experience any misery from anxiety! They're sure there's something dreadfully wrong with their relationship with Christ.

He continues, "You too must learn to accept anxious feelings as part of your human existence. You can get better, but you probably can't get totally 'over it,' because anxiety isn't a disease. It's a normal human emotion, part of life on this side of the resurrection."[2]

We shouldn't be surprised about troubles; otherwise we'll try to avoid them. Or, at the least, not think about them. Then a hidden anxiety will rumble around in our brain and affect us more than we realize. Like a cow chewing its cud, we let it ramble, rumble, and ruminate in our minds, and the result is distrust and unbelief in God's goodness and love.

That ruminating could even create an anxiety attack. Dr. Archibald Hart, in his book *The Anxiety Cure*, gives four solutions:

1. Don't run away from your symptoms. Face up to them.
2. Accept that what your body is doing for you is right for the moment. It may seem uncomfortable, but, like all pain, it is serving a purpose.
3. Give your panic a wide berth and allow it to pass. Other than taking control of your breathing, there is nothing you can do. Wait it out.
4. Keep reminding yourself that the attack is only a temporary interruption.[3]

Surprise Attack!

Although it didn't give me an anxiety attack, a "surprise" attack did throw me for a loop and created a lot of worry. It was one of my regular days of playing golf with the women at our local course, and

I couldn't believe how well I was playing. As a fairly new golfer of about three years, I had been improving steadily, and today—wow! We had finished four holes, and I was doing fabulous. I felt on top of my game.

As I walked with the other three women up to the fifth tee, one of the women, Eva (not her real name), looked at me quizzically and said, "You must be a sandbagger; you're playing too well for your handicap."

My voice caught in my throat, my thoughts a jumble, trying to sort through what she'd just said. *A sandbagger?* She's accusing me of cheating and lying? Though new to the game, I knew that a sandbagger was a person who tried to keep their handicap high (which can be good) by either playing poorly on purpose when not in a tournament or by not turning in their low scores (which would make their handicap lower). For those who don't play golf this may sound odd. But in golf, unlike other games, low scores indicate the best players.

Now as Eva looked innocently at me, I fumbled out explanations like, "I've been practicing a lot and taking lessons. My game has really improved."

Yet my words seemed so inadequate to try to refute her accusation. I felt even more confused, because she had said it in such a friendly way. Then it was my turn to hit the ball, and we all got into our golf carts and headed for our balls. The game continued, but my emotions were still back at the fifth tee. *She accused me of lying! How can I defend myself? How can I convince her I'm honest? I'm trying to represent Christ to these women; how can I protect my reputation if she is saying things like that?*

My thoughts were as scattered as if ten golfers had hit their balls at once and I was supposed to run around trying to retrieve them. The more I stewed over my inadequacy to answer her accusation, the more I started hitting balls all over the place. No matter how much I tried to tell myself, *Don't let her comment bother you,* the more my game dissolved. My final score was one of my worst in a long time.

Then last week I was playing in a golf tournament, and I was again doing well. My practice the previous day was paying off, and I felt more in control of my game than I had in a long time. Then it happened! One of the women I was playing with, asked, "Kathy, what is your handicap again? You sure are playing better than your handicap indicates."

My heart sank. I rehearsed Eva's comments from the past, and the emotions I battled then started to rise again. *Is this woman also accusing me of being a sandbagger?*

This time, however, I was ready. I thought, *No! I'm not going to let this bother me! I am improving in my game and I'm honest. Thank you, Lord, for Eva's comment months ago, because now I can handle this kind of comment!*

I continued playing well and won second place—I couldn't believe it! Eva's comment had served its purpose, and now I was protected from devastation when it really counted—in a tournament! When I spend my prize (a $50 gift certificate), I'm going to say, "Bless you, Eva!"

Don't be surprised when you experience trials. But be steadfast in resisting *worrying* about them. That's our next principle.

Do Be Steadfast!

First Peter 5:8–10 tells us,

> Be of sober spirit, be on the alert. Your adversary, the devil, prowls around like a roaring lion, seeking someone to devour. But resist him, firm in your faith, knowing that the same experiences of suffering are being accomplished by your brethren who are in the world. After you have suffered for a little while, the God of all grace, who called you to His eternal glory in Christ, will Himself perfect, confirm, strengthen and establish you.

The Amplified Bible explains "firm in your faith" as "rooted, established, strong, immovable, and determined." Satan wants to discourage our trust in God by flinging trials, problems, and persecutions at us, hoping we'll say, "Enough is enough! I'm not going to take any more. I'm worried things will get even worse." Even if we don't turn away from the Lord, we will be distracted and ineffective in our witness because we're too absorbed in worry.

Kitty Chappell gives us a wonderful way to resist Satan and be steadfast. She writes in *Sins of a Father: Forgiving the Unforgivable* about how she worried when she left her children at home when she accompanied her husband on trips for their business. Even though they were with capable baby-sitters, she envisioned all sorts of horrible things happening. But then something occurred that gave her the power to go in the opposite direction. She had to go to her chiropractor for an injured back and was in too much pain to relax long enough to receive an adjustment.

She writes,

> After a couple of unsuccessful attempts, he said, "Wiggle the toes on your right foot." When I wiggled my toes, he made the adjustment—without pain.
>
> "Why did I have to wiggle my toes?" I asked.
>
> "When you concentrated on wiggling your toes," he explained, "your focus shifted from your back pain to your toes. You relaxed, and I could make the adjustment."
>
> Driving home, I thought, *Why wouldn't the "wiggle your toes" principle work in other areas?* I had read or heard somewhere that worry is merely negative imagination. Could I break the chain of worry by substituting positive imagination for the negative? When we left on our next trip and the old negative thought patterns began to play, I changed tactics. I substituted positive "what ifs" for the usual negatives.
>
> What if, while we are gone, the baby-sitter is watching the children playing in the front yard and a kind white-haired gentleman walks by and stops to chat with them? He is a lonely widower with no children or grandchildren of his own. Our kids really take to him. The baby-sitter carefully observes him and decides he's just a harmless, kind, lonely old man who loves children. He chats with them for a while and then resumes his walk.
>
> I build this scenario to the point that when we return home, we become friends with the kind old man and adopt him into our family circle. Several years later he dies and leaves a fortune to our children. (And we had thought he was penniless!) Our children's college education was secured. Our son became a surgeon and our daughter an attorney.
>
> Wait a minute, my logical mind interjects. This is a stupid story! Just because you are gone on a business trip, you think that's going to happen? Not likely! But I, now knowing that I have the power to wiggle my mental toes and break the negative focus, reply, *That's true. But neither is it likely that my house is going*

to burn down just because I am gone.

After our second trip I was free of the negative worries—forever. I received more than a manipulation that freed me from physical pain that day at the chiropractor's office. I discovered a method of attitude adjustment that freed me from a lifetime of mental and emotional pain.[4]

Kitty saw "spring flowers" that came out of facing her fears, and so did author and speaker Janet Holm McHenry. She writes in *Daily PrayerWalk*,

As a child I'd had nightmares of falling and was afraid of heights in the daytime, too. A year ago when I visited Colorado Springs, I drove to the top of Pike's Peak in a tiny rental car. The road ascends eight thousand feet, winding around very tiny corners on the edge of precipitous cliffs. In fact, many of those drop-offs may have been thousands of feet. But I made it to the top, admittedly a little shaky. At the gift store at the 14,110-foot peak, I selected the T-shirt that would announce to the world that I had made it up and took it to a young man at a register.

"Do you ever have people who drive up here and can't go back down?" I asked.

He leaned over and whispered, "Are you one of those people?"

"Maybe," I whispered back.

When he told me I could make it back—in low gear—I decided maybe I *wasn't* one of those people. And I wasn't. Afterward I even climbed the 224 steps of the suspended staircase of Seven Falls—and back down in a lightning storm. Okay, I did hold up quite a few folks behind me going down, but . . . *I made it!*

Our God is greater than our fears.[5]

Our God *is* greater than our fears, and we can face our worries and allow God to stretch us! Then we'll see the spring flowers bloom from the rain.

Don't Resist Stretching

What accompanies worry? Things like lack of joy, disbelief, confusion, discontentment, and other destructive results. We don't want that! But if we can notice the bright, colorful blooms that come from going through problems and difficulties, we'll be less likely to let worry control us. As we said in chapter 1, "Hey, even if what I worry about does happen, God will make me a better person because of it. I don't have to fear troubles."

That's the point of James 1:2–8:

> Consider it all joy, my brethren, when you encounter various trials, knowing that the testing of your faith produces endurance. And let endurance have its perfect result, that you may be perfect and complete, lacking in nothing. But if any of you lacks wisdom, let him ask of God, who gives to all generously and without reproach, and it will be given to him. But he must ask in faith without any doubting, for the one who doubts is like the surf of the sea, driven and tossed by the wind. For that man ought not to expect that he will receive anything from the Lord, being a double-minded man, unstable in all his ways.

The people James addressed were under heavy persecution and had something legitimate to worry about. But James writes that they should think of trials and their potential worries with joy, knowing that there would be endurance, wisdom, and greater faith within them—the flowers that bloom after the rain.

If you're wondering whether James is writing only about persecution (and therefore these verses don't apply to your worries), let Charles Swindoll explain the meaning of the word *various*. He says it's the Greek word "from which we get the term polka dot. By this he [James] means that we can expect our lives to be spattered with trials of all sizes and shapes."[6]

Did you know you live a polka-dot life? You do. You face a variety of trials and tribulations, and they are all meant to be used by God to stretch you into the person He wants you to be. So whether you are worrying about a physical, emotional, or spiritual problem, this passage (James 1:2–8) applies to your situation.

Pastor Swindoll goes on to explain that the purpose of "testing" is to "approve" us before God. He says, "It's a word found on the undersides of many ancient pieces of pottery unearthed by archeologists in the Near East. This mark meant that the piece had gone through the furnace without cracking; it had been approved. God's desire is to help the clay vessels created in His image to mature in the furnace of trials without a crack."[7]

But do you know what can cause us to crack? Worry, for one thing—by not wanting or allowing troubles to mature us into someone God can use for His glory! If we resist stretching to become more like the person God wants us to be, He will just have to allow deeper trials—and that *is* something to worry about—we don't want that!

Rick Warren writes,

> Character building is a slow process. Whenever we try to avoid or escape the difficulties in life, we short-circuit the process, delay our growth, and actually end up with a worse kind of pain—the worthless type that accompanies denial and avoidance. When you grasp the eternal consequences of your character development, you'll pray fewer *"Comfort me"* prayers ("Help me feel good") and more *"Conform me"* prayers ("Use this to make me more like you.").[8]

A Many-Layered Process

I'd much rather say, "Comfort me" than "Conform me." For several years I've worried that God would "conform" me through the process of my taking care of my father-in-law, Don. I wondered if that would be the way God would eradicate the resentment I held toward him.

For the greater part of our marriage, Larry's father was involved in a cult. He didn't want to celebrate Christmas with our children, and he made our visits to his home filled with tension as he dogmatically spouted his ideas about religion. I felt angry that he hurt Larry's mother so deeply and that he wasn't the spiritually encouraging grandfather I wanted for Darcy and Mark.

Over the years I tried many times to forgive him, but it was a many-layered bitterness in which I went back and forth, forgiving him and then getting angry again. I cried out to God many times, saying, "Lord, I want to forgive him completely, but another layer of resentment keeps surfacing. Help me!"

Throughout those years, in the back of my mind, I thought, *I'll bet God is going to make it necessary for me to physically care for him in his old age. That will most likely make me become tender toward him. Will I be able to do it?*

Then, after twenty-seven years in the cult, Don turned back to believing that Jesus is the only way of salvation. In many ways he became a changed man. He was joyful and loving. I respected the courage it took for him to turn from his old thinking. But he never asked for forgiveness or acknowledged the hurt he had caused our family. I tried to accept that I most likely would never hear the words I wanted to hear from him: "I was wrong. I'm sorry, will you forgive me?" The thought continued to haunt me, *God will have me care for him so that I can truly forgive him.*

Then a month ago, only two weeks after we celebrated his ninetieth birthday, Don suffered a brain aneurysm and went into a deep coma. That was a Tuesday. As he hung on I could see the writing on the wall. Larry and I would soon be providing hospice care for him in our home! Larry and I were united in our desire to care for him as soon as we realized Don could no longer stay in the hospital because of a lack of insurance. It was all happening just as I had imagined (and worried) it would for many years.

In my devotional time I felt led to write Don a letter to try to clear away the bitterness so that I could care for him lovingly. I wrote,

> *Dad: I am very angry with you for dividing our family. I hated you for being so obstinate and opinionated. For being selfish, thinking only you had truth. For not being a listener and not showing concern for others. You hurt your own wife, you hurt your son, you hurt me, and you diminished a good relationship with your grandchildren because of your selfishness and self-focus. I am angry that you ruined our family closeness. For many years we couldn't approach you because you were so determined to spew your lies. You separated yourself and chose your religion over your family, studying in your room and going off to your services while we visited.*
>
> *Yet what is weird is that I respect and admire you for following what you thought was right even though it meant the misunderstanding of your family. Though you were wrong, you were faithful to what you thought was right—at a great cost. Yes, you did it out of pride and your own brand of compulsive personality, but you thought you were following God.*
>
> *Although you haven't acknowledged the pain and hurt you caused our family, you have tried in your own way to make up for the past. In turning back to the Lord you allowed God to make you a new creation— full of joy and enthusiasm and love for others. I want to forgive you and be cleansed of my anger, bitterness, and resentment toward you. I forgive*

you. I release needing you to acknowledge your error and its consequences. You did the best you could with the dysfunction within you. I release you from having to admit your error. O Lord, O God, help me to truly release and forgive him.

I paused and then continued writing, *"Dad, I will gladly care for you until you leave this earth. I love you. I care for you. Thank you for the gift of your son, who is precious, valuable, and important to me. We will miss you. I will miss you. I'm glad I will see you again in heaven. I release you."* I knew that God had done an important healing in me.

We arranged to bring Don to our home the next day for hospice care. But then the hospital called and said he could stay at the hospital after all. On Saturday we visited him. As he lay there comatose I leaned over him and whispered in his ear, *"I love you and I forgive you. You can go to Jesus in peace."*

The following Tuesday he did. I have felt no animosity toward him since writing that letter. Through the journey of forgiving him, layer after layer, I learned to steadfastly forgive again and again. This was a stretching experience for me, coming to a place where I could resist worrying about caring for him. Though I had previously feared it greatly, in the end I found I was more than willing to do it.

I don't know why God spared me from having to care for him, but I know I could have done it with love and care. I was no longer afraid. God brought spring flowers from the rain.

Even in the midst of fear and worry, we can trust God. We don't need to be surprised when problems assault us. We can stand steadfast, knowing that God will stretch us to become more like Christ.

What worry are you facing? Are you surprised by the attack? Can you stand firm, believing God will bring good from what you fear, even while you learn to trust Him more? I know that you can trust God to stretch you and in the process bring forth some amazingly beautiful spring flowers.

Abigail / 1 SAMUEL 25:1–42

In spite of being a God-fearing woman, Abigail had a lot to worry about, thanks to other important people in her life. But she faced her fear head on. As a result she was not only stretched to grow into an even more godly woman, but she also reaped great personal benefit from her experience.

She was married to Nabal, a "harsh and evil" man (1 Samuel 25:3), who was a drunkard. When he mistreated David and his men, who wanted to cross his land peacefully, David vowed to kill not only Nabal but all of his family and everything connected with him. When Abigail heard what had happened to David, the one whom everyone knew had been chosen to be the next king of Israel, she fearlessly went to him to seek peace and make amends if she could.

As she rode up to David, she may have been thinking, *I can't believe I'm doing this. Jehovah, are you sure this is what you want? Maybe I heard you wrong. David is already so angry. Will this bold maneuver make him even angrier? Oh, I hope not. Lord, give me favor with him!*

In spite of her fear she obeyed her God, and He gave her favor with David. Then she allowed God to stretch her even more as she returned to tell Nabal what she had done without his knowledge. Saving her from certain verbal abuse, if not physical abuse, God struck Nabal dead.

Some time later David remembered her kindness and wisdom in handling the crisis and asked her to become one of his wives—a proposal she gladly accepted. Her faith in God brought great benefit out of her trial. We want to be just like Abigail, and we can be!

 ## DISCUSSION QUESTIONS

1. What would you say is your natural reaction to troubles? To what degree are you surprised by them? Why do you think Peter believed that his readers were surprised at the onslaught of ordeals (1 Peter 4:12–13)?

2. Do trials ever feel "strange" to you? What do you think might be the reason?

3. How does believing "God isn't on the job" foster worry? Can you

think of a time you wondered if God had resigned from His position? What turned your thinking around?

4. How does my cheesecloth visual help you to trust God more?

5. Read 1 Peter 5:8–10 again. In what way does Satan gain victory over us most often? How can Kitty Chappell's "wiggle the toes" concept help you?

6. What fear could you face head on?

7. How does seeing the value of "stretching" help you to diminish the power of worry?

8. Read James 1:2–8 again. In the past, when you have faced trials with joy, what happened within you? In the circumstances?

9. Share a time that you "cracked" going through the furnace of worries, and another time when you were marked "approved" because of the way you handled your worry.

10. What are you currently worried about that will give you the opportunity to say "Conform me" rather than "Comfort me"?

11. Read 1 Samuel 25:1–42. What strikes you as remarkable about Abigail? In what way would you like to be more like her?

Letter from God

My Precious Daughter,

I never waste anything! Your trials and anything that makes you worry is something I intend to use. You are growing stronger in Me and in My power, and that's what life is all about. Don't be surprised when trials come. Only in heaven will there be nothing hard. The whole purpose of life on earth is to prepare you for joining Me in heaven. I am forming you into the image of My Son, Jesus, and your responses will ready you for the rewards I am planning here.

As you face any problem and challenge, see each one as an opportunity to stay steadfast and take the action I'm directing you to take. It's an opportunity to get stronger as you stare at Satan and say, "I'll continue to trust God no matter what! You can't make me doubt or distrust God's incredible love for me." That's what I want to hear.

Reaffirm at each difficulty that you believe that My love filter is still wrapped around you. There are no holes in My love filter. I only allow that which I intend to use for your good and My glory—to bring spring flowers.

Precious one, allow Me to stretch you. I promise to do it gently and tenderly, even when it seems overwhelming for you. I'm standing right there with you, wrapping your heart in My loving hands even when you're receiving bad news. I'm there! I'll never leave you nor forsake you.

I love you.

Your Heavenly Father

CHAPTER 7

Ice Storm

How to Keep Worry From Slipping Into Controlling Others

*I*t's not really funny, but there's something oddly humorous about watching cars slipping and sliding on ice through the white haze of a snowstorm on TV. It must be a horrible feeling to be so helpless and powerless. And I apologize for smiling as I see such destruction, but it's like a slapstick movie.

Sometimes we laugh about our tendency to worry too. But worry really isn't humorous, is it? We shouldn't treat it like a laughing matter, downplaying its destructive and sinful impact on our relationships.

Like those cars slipping on the ice, we can sometimes feel helpless and powerless in our attempts to motivate someone else to act right, think right, or do what we think they should do. And in our powerless state our common reaction is to worry. We know the other person isn't enjoying life. They may even be literally destroying themselves through their behavior. No wonder we're concerned! We know what's right for them, and they aren't cooperating with our wonderful ideas. Then it's easy to begin believing that

• worry communicates love;

- worry changes other people; and
- worry controls other people.

But worry, in fact, undermines our relationships. Let's look at these ideas in more detail.

Worry Can't Communicate Love

I talked with a woman at a women's retreat who could see this very thing in her own relationship with her mother. Vicki told me, "I can't stand the way my mother worries about me. I guess she thinks it means she loves me, but it just makes me feel like she's trying to control me."

Vicki frowned and then paused as if trying to sort through her thoughts. She looked at me intently, "I know what her worry does to me. It puts me back into being a little girl. She always tried to control me, and now that I'm a grown woman with a husband and children, I don't want to be her little girl! I'm an attorney, we own our home, and my daughters are in college. She calls me and asks me things like 'Did you remember to tell Kristy to get that class we talked about?'"

When she paused again I could tell she was getting angrier. "And do you know what else she does? When I drive her someplace, she tells me what streets to take, even though I've lived in the area for ten years. It makes me feel so . . . incompetent! That's it, Kathy! I hadn't put it into concrete thought before, but her worry makes me feel like I can't do anything!"

Vicki identified some important feelings and insights into her mother's efforts to control her daughter. Oh, did I say, "control"? Would Vicki's mother think she was trying to control her daughter? Most likely, she wouldn't.

What would Vicki's mother say about their relationship? I wonder if she would say. "Control? Oh no, not me! I'm just a mother *concerned* for her daughter and granddaughters. I think about what Vicki and I talked about—like Kristy's college class—and I just want to make sure she remembered our conversation. What's wrong with that? And the driving? Well, there's really no need for us to waste time if Vicki's forgotten how to get there. Come now! Control? I'm just being a mother."

I'm sure Vicki would be ready to tear out her hair if she heard her mother's explanation. She'd most likely say, "She doesn't have a clue!"

Vicki's mom's "concern" is fueled by fear and worry. Like a cow chewing its cud, she mulls over her daughter's and granddaughter's lives and tries to make sure they don't make any mistakes and aren't inconvenienced. But it's easy to see that worry is driving a wedge between these two women.

Just a few months ago Larry and I were driving along on our way to my brother's church for their Christmas Eve service. We had invited our son, Mark, who lives twenty miles away, to meet us there. We all (including Mark) used to live in the area of my brother's church before we moved two years ago. Mark called me on his cell phone to check on the time of the service, thinking it was much later than it actually was. After I told him the time, I began to give him driving instructions.

Okay, I knew well enough that it's the area where we lived before, but I didn't know if Mark knew where the church was located. Guess I should have asked, but I didn't. As I'm talking to Mark, Larry is whispering to me, "You're treating him like a two-year-old!"

ME? I'm just giving useful information. It wasn't until later that I recognized the obvious: I should have asked Mark, "The church meets at the Brea Community Center where we had Daddy's retirement party. Do you want directions?" Then the "control" ball would have been in his court, and I wouldn't have tried to communicate love through worry.

I didn't feel like I was worrying at the time, *but* I sure didn't want Mark to be late to the service. You see, I wanted him there to give God an opportunity to draw Mark closer to Him. Mark was already late, and I didn't want anything to prevent God from working on him. Is that worry? Well, maybe. But it was out of love!

And that's where we get into trouble. We begin to look at our fear and worry as stemming from love, and we slide on the thin ice of not trusting God. We need to know that love isn't spelled "w-o-r-r-y"!

For many years I wondered about that. I can still remember as a child hearing my grandmother say to me, "Kathy, I was worried about you." I have no clue or memory of what she might have been worried about, but I remember her comment. In my heart I believed she was trying to say, "I'm worried about you—I love you!" But what was even more meaningful, and brought me to tears, was the moment when I heard what I *really* wanted to hear: my grandmother telling me, "Kathy, I prayed for you."

Prayer is powerful, but worry is powerless. Prayer builds the relationship; worry destroys it. God never says, "I'm worried about you," but He does say, "I love you," and the Holy Spirit says, "I'm praying for you" (Romans 8:27).

We can believe that worry for our loved one does *something*—communicates love, at least—but that's not true.

Often we are unaware that people are hesitant to tell us things if they know we worry. And so we lose the opportunity to draw closer to others through honest communication. But if a person tells us, "I'll be praying about that," we are more apt to share our lives with them.

When I see a person who worries a lot I can predict that they will overreact to the people they love because of fear. Talk about a slippery slide on ice into wounded relationships! We all know the scenario. Our daughter is late getting home from a date. It's past her curfew, and worry begins to rear its ugly head with horrible thoughts of her being raped, or an automobile accident taking her life, or . . . a thousand other fears. We know those kinds of things can actually happen, and we're afraid it's going to happen to our family!

When our daughter walks in the door late because she and her date ran out of gas, what is our reaction? You guessed it—anger. "I've been so worried! How could you put me through this? What were you thinking? Couldn't you have called?"

Does this kind of angry outburst communicate love? No, it breaks down the relationship and creates fear within the child. Worry didn't keep her safe, and worry has now made her afraid. We can justify our worry by saying, "I love her. I don't want anything bad to happen to her." But that is only a rationalization to justify our lack of faith and dependence upon God. It may seem like the motherly thing to do, but it only creates friction in a relationship. We don't have to worry!

I don't know the author of this humorous bit of writing (it came to me over the Internet), but it might help us to pause and think about the lack of power worry has.

"When Do We Pass the Torch?"

Is there a magic cutoff period when offspring become accountable for their own actions? Is there a wonderful moment when parents can become detached spectators in the lives of their children and shrug—"It's their life"—and feel nothing?

When I was in my twenties, I stood in a hospital corridor waiting for doctors to put a few stitches in my daughter's head. I asked, "When do you stop worrying?" The nurse said, "When they get out of the accident stage." My mother just smiled faintly and said nothing.

When I was in my thirties, I sat on a little chair in a classroom and heard how one of my children talked incessantly, disrupted the class, and was headed for a career making license plates. As if to read my mind, a teacher said, "Don't worry, they all go through this stage and then you can sit back, relax, and enjoy them." My mother just smiled faintly and said nothing.

When I was in my forties, I spent a lifetime waiting for the phone to ring, the cars to come home, the front door to open. A friend said, "They're trying to find themselves. Don't worry, in a few years you can stop worrying. They'll be adults." My mother just smiled faintly and said nothing.

By the time I was fifty, I was sick and tired of being vulnerable. I was still worrying over my children, but there was a new wrinkle: There was nothing I could do about it. My mother just smiled faintly and said nothing.

I continued to anguish over their failures, be tormented by their frustrations, and absorbed in their disappointments. My friends said that when my kids got married I could stop worrying and lead my own life. I wanted to believe that, but I was haunted by my mother's warm smile and her occasional, "You look pale. Are you all right? Call me the minute you get home. Are you depressed about something?"

Can it be that parents are sentenced to a lifetime of worry? Is concern for one another handed down like a torch to blaze the trail of human frailties and the fears of the unknown? Is concern a curse or is it a virtue that elevates us to the highest form of life?

One of my children became quite irritable recently, saying to me,

"Where were you? I've been calling for three days and no one answered. I was worried."

I smiled a warm smile. The torch has been passed.[1]

We don't have to pass the torch! We don't have to worry! It doesn't do any good, and it doesn't communicate love. Grab hold of trust in God to prevent this slide on ice.

Worry Can't Change Others

Worry doesn't communicate love, but there's still something deep inside of us that believes worry can *change* others. If someone we love has a different perspective than we do, we worry. If someone we love has a different belief about God, we worry. If someone we love has a character flaw, we worry. We just know their wrong thinking will mess up their lives!

And some of these worries may truly seem "worthy" of worry. Your mother may not know Christ as her Savior, and she has cancer. Your son may be on the street taking drugs. Your friend may demonstrate a lack of integrity at work. Another friend drives while intoxicated. You may have tried to reason, cajole, quote Scripture, even manipulate each person into changing their ideas and their behavior, but nothing has worked—not even prayer. God hasn't changed them either! You fear that something bad, really bad, is going to happen. Your faith is fishtailing on ice.

Even if it's not a matter of something really bad occurring, we can easily take responsibility for someone else's happiness and then respond in an unhealthy way. I'm recognizing that possibility right now as we walk through the grief process with Larry's mother.

As I mentioned in chapter 6, Larry's father passed away a month ago at the age of ninety. Larry's parents, Don and Audrey, were married for sixty-two years, and in that time Audrey was alone overnight for fewer than twenty nights—total! Even when Don was away during two different wars, Audrey's mother lived with her so she wasn't alone. As recently as four or five months ago Audrey remarked to me, "If something happens to Don, I don't know if I can live alone." Then about a month later she commented, "I've been thinking about living alone and I think I can do it." I was so proud of her.

The first night of Don's hospitalization, Audrey stayed in our home. The next day she surprised us with her spunk, saying she wanted to return to her own home. I volunteered to spend the night at her home, but she said, "No, I have to get used to it." And she did! Since that night she has been in her own home.

But that doesn't mean I haven't worried about her loneliness. During the first two weeks we made sure she had something to do with us every day. But realizing we couldn't keep that up for long, especially as I began to write this book, I wondered how she would cope.

In my prayer time I prayed verses for Audrey dealing with the topic of loneliness. I began praying Psalm 146:9 for her: "The LORD protects the strangers; He supports the fatherless and the widow, But He thwarts the way of the wicked." Unexpectedly, I thought, "I shouldn't try to fill the place the Lord wants in her life." Wow—that hit me hard! In my worry about her loneliness, I had begun to feel responsible to make sure she wasn't lonely. I wrote in my journal, "I can try to be there too much and she could depend upon me and/or Larry instead of looking to you, Lord. Help me, Father, to resist the compulsion to 'be there' for her too much."

When I told Larry about what the Lord had revealed to me, I jokingly (but with some seriousness) quipped, "God doesn't want me to be your mom's grief savior." If I had continued to worry about her I could have easily become that. And I'd be good at it because I so easily take responsibility for the happiness of others.

When I talked to Audrey later that day, she enthusiastically said, "Guess what Chuck Swindoll talked about on his radio program today?"

"What, Mom Audrey?"

"Loneliness! It really ministered to me."

I laughed. God had come through! I didn't need to be in charge of making sure she wasn't lonely. Of course she's going to be lonely—she's alone for the first time in her life! We certainly are going to help her, but she should primarily look to God, not us. Otherwise, she'll draw too close to us and not closer to God.

If you are slipping on the thin ice of taking responsibility for the happiness of others, or trying to change the opinions and beliefs of others, remember these verses:

The first is: "No man can by any means redeem his brother or give to God a ransom for him" (Psalm 49:7). You cannot save anyone else. Although we can share our faith, quote Scripture, and be an example, the choice to become a Christian is in the control of the other person.

Prayer is the most effective and powerful means of encouraging someone to receive Christ as their Savior. My favorite verse to pray for unbelievers is, "'Open their eyes so that they may turn from darkness to light and from the dominion of Satan to God, that they may receive forgiveness of sins and an inheritance among those who have been sanctified by faith in Me [Christ]'" (Acts 26:18).

The second is: "Let us therefore, as many as are perfect, have this attitude; and if in anything you have a different attitude, God will reveal that also to you" (Philippians 3:15). If God has the ability to give you and me a different attitude, He can do it for anyone. He is powerful and creative. When we worry or feel like we have to change someone's ideas, we are saying, "God, you aren't effective enough. You aren't creative enough to work in this person's life. I've got to do it myself."

When I think of how God creatively worked in our daughter Darcy's life, I sense the tears coming. I've already shared with you how God used Larry's melanoma to heal our relationship with her. But God also created circumstances that encouraged an even closer relationship several years later.

Darcy went to Denmark for a semester of college and requested to live in the home of a Danish family. Soon our phone calls were centered on how badly her Danish "mother" was treating her—ignoring her and saying mean things to her. Larry and I were incensed, as most parents would be, and I began to worry about my daughter's emotional health. Then my worry fueled anger toward this woman who had no right to treat *my* daughter like that! We suggested Darcy move to on-campus housing, but she wanted to stick it out. Since we couldn't afford to go visit her (I would have loved to give that woman a piece of my mind), I had to stew over it . . . in the beginning.

Then I began to see God's work in Darcy's life because of her circumstances. She began to appreciate our family as she never had before; in comparison to the way her Danish family treated her, we were looking pretty good. In fact, fabulous! I'd never heard as much love and warmth in Darcy's voice as when we talked with her. Shortly before she returned home she sent a Christmas card and wrote in it:

> *Dear Dad, Mom, and Mark:*
>   *Since I can't be there with you for Christmas, I'm writing to tell you how much I'll miss not being there and how much I love you all. Being away has really made me realize how awesome a family you are. I love and appreciate all of you so much!! I can't wait to come home to see you all. Give my love to the rest of the family. I'll be seeing you on January 6.*
> *Love, Darcy*

That was in 1994. After Darcy returned, her appreciation for our family continued to rise to great heights, and it all started with something I was worried about. It's every mother's longing to have her child value their family. But in our case, God accomplished this through mistreatment, something I would have changed if I could. But if I had, the good results God intended would not have occurred. Even today, when we talk about that situation, Darcy remarks, "Oh yes, God really used that in my life."

We don't want to thwart God's changes in those we love, do we? We need to make sure that worry doesn't prevent His work. Let's live like we believe God *can* change others.

Worry Can't Control Others

I can't tell you how often I've thought, *If only he would . . .* or *If she will just . . .* I admit, at times I've tried to control other people. I've even tried to control them through prayer. Yes, we're supposed to pray, but we're not supposed to try to *control* them through prayer. Here comes that icy slope again!

You probably remember my sharing how I prayed that Larry would become a quadriplegic so that he would stay home—that's a good example of trying to control someone through prayer. But I also prayed during that time, "God, make his plane crash!"

Larry had gone off on another flying trip, leaving me alone with a two-year-old and an infant, and I was not a happy camper. I was controlled by anger, convinced that he was insensitive to my needs. Since I constantly nagged and criticized him, it's no wonder he wanted to be gone as much as possible.

By the way, have you ever thought of worry as the source of some of our nagging and criticism? Somehow we think that our nagging and criticism will control the other person. Maybe we're feeling insecure about our husband's love. *Does he still love me?* And so we nag, trying to get any response, even if it's negative. *At least he's paying attention to me!*

I couldn't even get Larry to pay attention to me. He was gone so much with two jobs—being a policeman and a real estate agent—and his flying hobby that he was seldom home. It occurred to me that things wouldn't be too different for me if he were to die. So I prayed that the plane he was flying would crash—can you imagine? What selfishness—fueled by anger and worry. And what was I thinking? Did I think I could tell God what to do?

Neil Anderson says, "When you seek to play the role of the Holy Spirit in another person's life, you will misdirect that person's battle with God onto yourself."[2] I tried to play the role of the Holy Spirit in Larry's life and only made things worse. Thankfully, God doesn't say yes to every prayer we pray! Otherwise, I wouldn't have the wonderful, loving husband I do—the one who is right now taking his mother to the grocery store so that I can write.

Is your worry motivating you to try to gain control of someone? Maybe your worry for that person's health, salvation, or well-being is causing you to "rescue" them. One elderly woman came up to me after I spoke and said with tears streaming down her face, "I've been so worried about my grandson. I didn't want him to land on the streets homeless, so I've paid for his apartment and food for three years. I thought I was motivating him to get a job, but now I see that my worry has caused me to rescue him. I'm not going to do it anymore!"

As I shared Proverbs 19:19 with that woman, she became even more convinced that she needed to stop rescuing her grandson, no matter how worried she was about him. Proverbs 19:19 tells us, "A man of great anger will bear the penalty, for if you rescue him, you will only have to do it again."

Neither worrying nor rescuing does any good; it only brings destruction. Think of it this way: He (or she) needs to be needy so that he/she will need God. When they are needy, we can actually rejoice in that person's difficulties. Looking at it that way will stop our slide on ice!

Many times the reason we are motivated to control someone is because we're worried that he or she is a reflection of us, communicating in what they say or do something about our value or importance. Nowhere is this more apparent than in parenting.

When I was a young mother, I thought Darcy's behavior was a reflection of my worth and competence. When she had a temper tantrum on the grocery store floor, I worried that everyone observing her was thinking that I was a bad mom. In fact, I believed I could read the elderly woman's mind who walked by—I just knew she was thinking as she looked at Darcy, *Bad child*. And then she looked at me and thought, *Bad mom*. Because of those fears, I usually overreacted toward Darcy and hit her hard on her bottom to try to make her stop the behavior. But my fear and anger only made matters worse.

In time, I could see that Darcy wasn't a reflection of me. My worth and value were not connected to how she behaved. If I had whispered in her ear moments before her temper tantrum, "Now would be a good time for a temper tantrum," I would be responsible for her behavior. But guess what: I didn't do that! She made a choice to have a "TT," and it didn't mean I was a bad person; it meant that she was strong-willed. In time I learned to calmly respond to her with effective disciplinary techniques.

Jesus is our wonderful example of not taking His disciples' behavior personally. By the world's definition ("A child is a reflection of his parent.") Jesus should have been wringing His hands when His disciples failed Him.

When they were unsuccessful at casting out demons, Jesus could have worried, "Oh no! What are people thinking of me? I sure didn't train these disciples very well—they can't do what I've told them they can do." And when Peter denied Him, and Judas betrayed Him, Jesus didn't blame himself. He didn't worry about His own worth and value. He attributed His disciples' inadequacies to their own lack of growth and maturity and did not take their failures personally. We should follow His example!

If you are worried because the woman you are counseling or mentoring is still struggling in some sin, release your worry. She is not a reflection of you, and her slow process is her concern. If you are worried because your husband is involved in Internet pornography, release your worry. He's not a reflection of you; it's his obsession with trying to meet his needs in wrong ways that is the issue. If you are worried because your child is involved in drug abuse or homosexuality, release your worry. He or she is not a reflection of you; it's his or her own struggle.

Yes, God might call you to take some action in each of these situations, but don't "rescue" them and don't try to control their behavior. Instead, pray and set appropriate boundaries. And don't let worry fuel anger that leads to overreactions. You are only responsible for your responses—not theirs—in each situation.

Can you see worry's destructive results, how it causes you to respond inappropriately to other people? Can you see how expressing worry about somebody isn't the same as love? Can you see how worry may be fueling a need to control or change someone else?

You don't have to slide on that slippery ice. You don't have to pass the torch of worry. You can pray instead, committing that person to God and asking Him to work in his or her life. God is able and creative. Trust Him to work things out for good.

Salome / MATTHEW 20:20–24

Salome, mother of James and John, had a lot to worry about. Think of it this way. You're already rich. You already can give your children everything they want. You're respected in the community, married to a successful businessman. There's nothing else you can give your children, because they have it all. Except . . . spiritual greatness and honor. Why not aim for the top? Why not see your sons sitting at the right and left side of the future spiritual leader of the world?

But wait a minute—there's that other guy, Peter, who seems to be the spiritual leader's favorite. You don't want *him* to get the honors *your* sons deserve. You've been bothered by that Peter guy, and it's really concerning you that he might get that honor, leaving out your sons. This is not good. This is a worry! What can you do to see that the right people are put in the right places? And then you come up with the idea: "I'll talk to Jesus and ask Him to give the honor to my sons!"

We don't know if Salome (the name most commentators agree on for the mother of the "sons of Zebedee") was motivated by worry to make her request to Jesus. Maybe she worried that Peter would edge into the position she desired for her sons and get the honor she thought they deserved. Maybe she worried that the money and effort she'd invested in Jesus' ministry wouldn't get the results she desired. We can't really say for sure what fueled her question, but this is what she said to Jesus: "Command that in Your kingdom these two sons of mine may sit one on Your right and one on Your left" (Matthew 20:20–21).

The response was immediate by Jesus ("This is not Mine to give"). More importantly, though, the reaction from the other ten disciples was also immediate. "And hearing this, the ten became indignant with the two brothers" (Matthew 20:23–24). OUCH!

Was that her desire? Most likely not. Did she regret her actions? Most likely she did. Possibly fueled by worry, her question was inappropriate and brought adverse results. Yet in the distant future her desire *was* granted. Both her sons were martyred for their faith in Jesus, receiving the "drink" of His cup.

Salome tried to control Jesus, and it didn't reap the rewards she desired. We can learn from her example—that controlling others won't get us what we want either. We don't want to be like Salome, and we don't have to be!

 ## DISCUSSION QUESTIONS

1. When you think of someone you are worried about, who comes to mind first? Why?

2. Before you read this chapter, what would you have said about each of these three concepts:

   - Worry communicates love.
   - Worry changes other people.
   - Worry controls other people.

   In what way(s) have you believed these concepts in the past?

3. When someone expresses worry about you, how does it make you feel?

4. Can you think of a time when your expression of love was mistaken for worry? Did you do anything to correct the misperception?

5. How could Romans 8:27 help you to worry less?

6. Make a little sign of the phrase "Love Isn't Spelled W-O-R-R-Y" and place it in a conspicuous place.

7. How have you seen worry diminish one of your relationships (or someone else's)?

8. I mention several disadvantages of thinking that worry communicates love. For each one, give your impressions and how you fight against that false belief:

   - Worry makes people feel incompetent and controlled.
   - Worry makes people avoid telling us their concerns.
   - Worry makes me overreact.

9. Have you "passed the torch" of worry? If so, how do you plan to stop it? If not, good for you!

10. How does Psalm 49:7 speak to you?

11. Reread Philippians 3:15. Claim that promise for a specific concern about someone's wrong perspective (someone you worry about).

12. What did you think about the idea that nagging and criticism could be a result of worry? Can you identify that happening

within you at all? What does Proverbs 25:24 have to say?

13. Why do we sometimes think that we can be a better "Holy Spirit" than the Holy Spirit? How can we correct that tendency?

14. Can you remember a time when you rescued someone because of your worry over them? What happened? How has your perspective changed, or how does it need to change? How can Proverbs 19:19 empower you to stop rescuing?

15. Do you relate to Salome at all? If so, how? What will you do about it?

Letter from God

My Precious Daughter,

I understand your concern and care for other people. You truly do want what's best for them. You love that person and don't want them to hurt or suffer as a result of his or her choices. But think about this: What if the only way they will change is if I allow them to go through hard times? It would be worth it, wouldn't it? I know you don't want to prevent their transformation.

So let Me have My perfect way in them. It'll take all your trust in Me to stand by and let Me work, but I love them more than you do! Did you hear me, dear one? I love them more than you do. I know that might be hard to imagine. You love them with your whole heart, don't you? Well, so do I, and My heart is bigger than yours! Don't you think I'll do everything possible to draw them closer to My loving heart? I promise you, I will.

So let Me work. Get ready to see My creativity. I most likely won't do what you think I should. But I see the bigger picture. I see your loved one's heart, soul, and mind. I know their motives and their wounded heart. I created them, and I know what will draw them to Me.

Yes, it's going to take time. I know that waiting is hard. But there is always enough time for Me to work. I'm working even now; trust Me. I love them. I want what's best for them . . . and for you!

I love you.

Your Heavenly Father

CHAPTER 8

Rain Behind You

How the Past Can Cloud the Present

I loved driving! As a new driver with my driver's permit at the ripe old age of fifteen and a half, I begged for any opportunity to drive. My father, who had nerves of steel, always accompanied me, and I appreciated his calm demeanor. No matter what mistake I made, he calmly instructed me and seemed to enjoy my enthusiasm. It was so much fun to have this awesome responsibility. And it brought me attention!

One evening I drove into the church parking lot for a youth group meeting. Several of the boys were standing around. One of them was my current heartthrob, Robert Gene Smith, Jr. He was standing with his buddy, Terry, and when they saw me driving in, they gasped, threw up their arms in mock terror, and climbed onto Robert's car for protection. I laughed hysterically. *I love it! Hey, I'll take any attention, even if it's terror!*

Later that evening, at the end of the youth activity, my father brought the car to pick me up, and I hopped into the driver's seat after he slid over. "Thanks, Dad!" I exclaimed as I put the car into gear and carefully pulled out of the church parking lot. As I drove down the side street toward the stop sign, I remembered I hadn't gone through my pre-driving pattern of adjusting the rearview mirror. I began to fiddle with it, when suddenly my attention was brought back to the street and the cars in front of me! I slammed on the brakes and thankfully stopped with an inch or two to spare.

I gasped, "Whew! That was a close call. I'm glad I stopped in time."

My father spoke up. "Kathy, you stopped in time because I put my foot on the brake. You shouldn't have taken so much time looking in the rearview mirror."

"No, Dad!" I protested. "*I* stopped the car! I did it in time!"

My father slowly wagged his head. "No, Kathy, I did it! Be more careful next time. Adjust your rearview mirror before you start driving."

I couldn't believe him! I pouted all the way home, believing he wasn't telling the truth.

A year later, as I reviewed that incident, I was shocked that I had actually thought my father would lie to me. What possible purpose would he have in doing that? It was so different from his character. I've long regretted my reaction, but I never thought of asking his forgiveness before he died twenty-eight years ago.

Regrets are like constantly reviewing the rain behind us as we adjust our rearview mirror, putting us in danger of hitting the cars in front of us. Regrets are a dangerous form of worry, and so is another hazardous mental occupation: bitterness.

If worry is to mull over and over again a fear or concern about the future, then regrets are worry over something we did in the past; bitterness is worry over something someone else did in the past. Both regret and bitterness can create a car accident as we stare too long into the rearview mirror of life.

Sometimes we don't correctly identify regrets and bitterness as forms of worry. It's not worrying about the future—which is what we primarily think of as worry—but it's worrying about the past. Worrying about the future is the "What if's . . ." Regrets are the "If only's . . ." "If only I had been a better mother. . . ." or "If only she hadn't done that to me. . . ." We continue to think over and over about how life could be better now *if only* we had done something different in the past.

But regrets and bitterness are sin, just like any form of worry, because they both represent a state of discontent and a lack of trust in God. What can we do to fight against these forms of worry that keep us looking in the rearview mirror?

Remember, But Don't Regret

The apostle Paul could easily have struggled with regrets. He certainly had a lot to regret and also a lot to be bitter about toward others. For himself, he was instrumental in helping to persecute and kill Christians. Then, after coming to know Christ, he was misunderstood and rejected by Christians.

Yet he was able to write, "Not that I have already obtained it or have already become perfect, but I press on so that I may lay hold of that for which also I was laid hold of by Christ Jesus. Brethren, I do not regard myself as having laid hold of it yet; but one thing I do: forgetting what lies behind and reaching forward to what lies ahead, I press on toward the goal for the prize of the upward call of God in Christ Jesus" (Philippians 3:12–14).

Paul had learned the secret of overcoming regrets and bitterness: Forget the past and reach forward to the future. We could easily misunderstand his intent if we're not careful. He's not saying we should be able to wipe a memory out of our minds. Warren Wiersbe explains, "Please keep in mind that in Bible terminology, 'to forget' does not mean 'to fail to remember.' Apart from senility, hypnosis, or a brain malfunction, no mature person can forget what has happened in the past. We may wish that we could erase certain bad memories, but we cannot. 'To forget' in the Bible means 'no longer to be influenced by or affected by.'"[1]

Paul is not saying that his readers shouldn't remember the past, or he wouldn't have rehearsed the past as he did earlier in the third chapter of Philippians. What he is saying is that Christians shouldn't be held captive by the past, which could include past accomplishments, past heritage, past sins that have been forgiven, or past hurts that others have done to them.

Beth Moore explains,

Many well-meaning Christians take out of context the exhortation in Philippians 3:13, "forgetting what is behind," and apply it as a command to never look at the past. Paul was talking about all the trophies of life he had to leave behind to follow Christ. God's Word clearly expresses what a good and effective teacher the past can be. The past will be a good teacher if we will approach it as a good student, from the perspective of what we can gain and how God can use it for his glory.[2]

Actually, there is value in remembering the past. Remembering our sins keeps us humble and dependent upon God. Yet as in Paul's example of a runner, we want to be like that athlete who is concentrating so hard on the goal ahead that he isn't looking around to see where the other runners are. To do so would slow him down. Worry slows us down in our "race" of trusting God each day.

My friend Lynn Morrissey (author of *Love Letters to God*) told me a story of how looking in the rearview mirror of regrets created a wrong perspective about how God uses her. Besides being a writer, she is also an accomplished professional church soloist. But one Sunday all professional decorum melted as her high C collided with the organ's piercing C-sharp. Though it was her error, she had no recourse "mid song" but to sustain the glaring wrong note.

After the service, a beautiful, radiant woman named Grace lavished upon Lynn what Lynn believed was "undeserved praise." Embarrassed and with eyes downcast, Lynn lamented, "But, Grace, didn't you hear that awful note I caterwauled?"

Without hesitation Grace encouraged her, "Lynn, how many right notes did you sing?"

Lynn was dumbfounded. *How many right notes have I sung? Hundreds? Thousands? Hundreds of thousands?* she wondered. *And I'll be singing even more right notes in the songs that I sing in the future.*

Suddenly the truth of what Grace was trying to point out washed over her. Knowing her perfectionistic bent, Lynn knew that without Grace's comment she would have continued to regret and worry about her one wrong note. As a result, she would have been sour-faced and depressed for the rest of the day. She'd seen the pattern before, yet had never seen the destructive power of regretting a wrong note.

At the moment of Grace's comment, God's grace seemed so evident that Lynn decided not to let regret steal her joy.

What are you regretting? I know the feeling. I've regretted that I wasn't a better mom. I've regretted that I abused Darcy and was impatient with Mark. I've regretted the times I've been frustrated with Larry and not appreciated the great man he is. I've regretted my uncompassionate responses to friends. I've regretted not taking opportunities to share Christ when God prompted me to do so.

But I can't go back! You can't go back! Nothing, not even worry in the form of regret, will change the past. Someone has said, "Worry is the darkroom in which 'negatives' are developed." That's what our regrets do. They stir up the ingredients for a negative view of life. How can we stop looking in the rearview mirror of regret and bitterness?

Remember, But Forgive

The key is to forgive. Forgive ourselves and forgive others. No, we may not be able to forget, but we *can* forgive. Rick Warren writes, "Guilt-driven people are manipulated by memories. They allow their past to control their future. . . . We are products of our past, but we don't have to be prisoners of it. God's purpose is not limited by your past."[3]

Forgiveness releases the regrets and bitterness of life. Forgiveness is a choice to let go of focusing on the hurt that we inflicted upon ourselves or that others inflicted upon us. It's changing our thinking from "If only I. . . ." to "Next time I will. . . ." when regrets assail us. And it's changing our thinking from "I hate her for. . . ." to "I'm no longer going to try to punish her for. . . ."

For instance, if you said something hurtful to someone, you might be thinking, *If only I had been more helpful.* You can forgive yourself by asking your friend's forgiveness. Then think, *Next time, I'll look at it from that person's perspective.*

Or if you were angry at your daughter, you are most likely thinking, *If only I hadn't yelled at her.* Instead, forgive yourself by asking her forgiveness and then think, *Next time, I'll walk away first and come back to speak to her when I'm calm.*

In a similar manner, make the same choice for any resentment or bitterness toward others. When you remember someone's offense or the way he or she hurt you, instead of looking in the rearview mirror and rehearsing the hurt, change your thinking to *I can't change what they did to me. God will judge them. But I can choose to release them of my need to punish them.*

Is that easy to do? Absolutely not! After all, we're hurting, and we may be suffering the consequences of their choices. They may have done it maliciously, intending to hurt us, or it may have been an unfortunate mistake. Even if it was only a mistake, we can think, *If only they had been more careful.* No, it's not easy to forgive. But ask yourself, "Is my bitterness or resentment helping me? Is it gaining for me what I need?"

Bitterness and resentment continue your pain! You may be thinking, *I'm getting back at them with my negative thinking,* but think about it—the person who hurt you is off on his or her merry way, oblivious to your negative thinking. Stephen Harnock once observed, "Bitterness is like drinking poison and waiting for the other person to die."[4]

That's why God wants you to forgive others and yourself. It's poison either way. Paul wrote, "Do not grieve the Holy Spirit of God, by whom you were sealed for the day of redemption. Let all bitterness and wrath and anger and clamor and slander be put away from you, along with all malice. Be kind to one another, tender-hearted, forgiving each other, just as God in Christ also has forgiven you" (Ephesians 4:30–32). God wants only the best for you, and He knows that the poison of bitterness and resentment hurts you and no one else.

When we become convinced we must forgive, we can *make the decision* to do so. No, it won't feel good and it won't be easy, but you can do it by thinking (or preferably saying out loud), "I forgive (name of person)." You can apply this to yourself for your regrets too.

Once you make that decision to forgive yourself or someone else, know that it's like peeling an onion. There will be many layers to take off. If the old feelings of bitterness or resentment return, that doesn't mean you haven't forgiven that person. It just means you need to peel off another layer of bitterness by making that choice again and again.

Is it possible? Yes, I know it is. I was filled with regrets about the way I treated Darcy during that time when I physically and verbally abused her as a two-year-old. As I shared in chapter 1, I constantly yelled at her, at times kicking her and hitting her in the head; one time I even choked her. She cowered when I raised my hand innocently to scratch my head. It broke my heart to know she was terrified of me.

Even after God gave me the patience to be the loving mom I wanted to be and Darcy started trusting my love for her, I still agonized over the mental and emotional damage I'd done. *I've done so much damage; there's no way Darcy can grow up as an emotionally healthy adult. She's experienced so much fear already! Can we really have a good relationship? She may never forgive me completely!*

My wondering about this turned into fretting, and then into regret. I was horrified as I remembered the painful things I'd done to her. The images of hurting her constantly rumbled in my mind. *Can God heal Darcy? Can I forgive myself for what I've done?*

I also wondered if God could forgive me. I *knew* intellectually that child abuse could be forgiven but I couldn't *feel* God's forgiveness. That fueled my tendency to constantly look in the rearview mirror of regrets.

Then one day I was flipping through my Bible and noticed a verse I'd never seen before. "I, even I, am the one who wipes out your transgressions for My own sake, And I will not remember your sins" (Isaiah 43:25). As I meditated on that verse I was struck by the phrase, "for My own sake." I whispered, "You mean, God, that you want to wipe out my sin, not just for my benefit, but for yours too?"

That amazed me. God benefited in some way by forgiving me. *How, God?* And then I realized, *You want to have fellowship with me because you love me so much. And if there is unconfessed, and thus unforgiven, sin within me, you can't have fellowship with me.*

That meant so much! God gained from forgiving me. By refusing to forgive myself and rejecting His forgiveness, I was taking away that blessing.

From then on, each time I began to regret afresh my reactions toward Darcy, I remembered that verse. It set me free from thinking I couldn't be forgiven and couldn't forgive myself. God *wanted* to forgive me; not just wanted, but *longed* to do so! He felt blessed when He could forgive me so that we could enjoy fellowship. But I still didn't know if God could heal Darcy.

Several years later my first book was published. In it I told the story of how God had delivered me from being a child abuser. Darcy was in fifth grade at the time, and was so excited about her mother being an author that she asked, "Mom, can I take your book to school with me and show it to my teacher?"

I cringed. *Do I want Darcy's teacher to know about what happened with Darcy and me?* I decided that if Darcy felt comfortable taking it, I should too. Several months later when the book was returned (and we later found out that not only Darcy's teacher had read it but also several other teachers and the principal), there was a note from Darcy's teacher attached to it, which read, "I really love your daughter. She's a healthy, well-adjusted little girl."

I started crying when I read it. God had done the miracle of healing Darcy, even though I'd hurt her and worried about her emotional health. Today Darcy is a wonderful married woman who loves God and . . . *me*! All that I'd fretted about and regretted never brought the bad results I feared. Instead, God brought about a fabulous relationship between us and a ministry of hope to others.

Is there something that you regret? Is it hard to forgive yourself, or to forgive someone else? Know that God wants you to forgive yourself and other people for your benefit—and His. You can't forget what happened to you. But you can remember and forgive. Then you won't be looking in the rearview mirror of regrets and bitterness.

Remember, But Look Forward

Regrets and bitterness can easily fill our lives, especially if we've lived a long time. The longer we've driven through life and seen the rain in the rearview mirror, the more our vision can be clouded with regrets and bitterness. Yet I was amazed to read the perspective of Shirley Carson, who at sixty-four years young, could "remember and look forward."

She wrote to me,

> Recently I saw a sign that read, "Don't fret about aging; it's an opportunity many do not have." Society lies to us about old age, telling us that aging is awful. While certain aspects of it are admittedly very difficult, it is sad the entire focus seems to be on

the decline of the body and/or mind, and the dependence that follows.

The potential gifts of aging are rarely mentioned, such as a huge spirit, an ability to love without holding back, wisdom, courage, hope, trust, gratitude, and forgiveness. Perhaps the best gift of aging is becoming a mentor for others. The knowledge of how to experience both a good life and a good death can be passed on.

During the aging process we may experience many losses that we need to grieve. When we are willing to let go of things we are attached to, God fills us with more of Himself. He guides us through our lives that we may become all He has called us to be. So let us be grateful for this journey we are on. And let us not worry about aging, for it is indeed an opportunity many do not have.

Shirley has made an interesting distinction. She says we must grieve, but we don't need to have regrets. Grieving is important and necessary in order to process loss, but regrets are destructive and unnecessary. We can allow ourselves to feel the loss of unfulfilled expectations, but turning them into regrets doesn't bring back those opportunities. Grieving will eventually bring us to the point of looking ahead, but regrets keep us focused on the past.

That was God's message through the prophet Isaiah when he wrote, "Forget the former things; do not dwell on the past. See, I am doing a new thing! Now it springs up; do you not perceive it? I am making a way in the desert and streams in the wasteland" (Isaiah 43:18–19 NIV).

God doesn't want us to be "yesterday" people; He wants us to be "today" and "tomorrow" people, because that's how we get vision. Paul Faulkner said, "Don't waste a lot of today's energy trying to untangle lines that got tangled in your yesterdays. Cut line and get back to fishing."[5]

That's Jean Stewart's perspective too, even though she could be filled with regrets about the past. Like any mother, she wanted the best for her children and remembers the time she asked friends to pray that her daughter's greatest wish would be fulfilled: to be on the cheerleading and song-leading team. Her daughter practiced and worked hard to excel, but she didn't make the squad for two years—a very long time in high school. So Jean asked her Covenant group for their prayers once again, and recalls one of them saying, "Can't we just pray for her to want to do something else?"

Adamant about helping her young one succeed at whatever she wanted, Jean arranged for a professional cheerleader (one her family had watched on television during major football games) to coach her daughter. Jean says,

> It worked. My meddling was successful. Oh, what joy when her name was the first one called! She was thrilled. But the excitement lasted about a week. Then reality set in. Practice and games consumed all her spare time and left none for her beloved horseback riding. She soon discovered that most of the girls were "party girls," not keeping to the Christian standards that she had been raised to uphold. She didn't belong. She was never accepted. She worked with them but there was no joy, no delight, no fun. My meddling to ensure her win actually caused her to lose what she most enjoyed in life during that year.

Yet many years later Jean is not mired in regrets. She writes,

> Now that our daughter is grown, married, and a professional adult, I listen to her, try hard to advise only when asked, and, of course, continue to ask for prayers on her behalf. But I ask for God's will in her life—not mine. I learned my lesson well. Worry? I pray and work hard at "letting go and letting God" handle my life and those of my children and husband. With it comes a wonderful peace, free from regrets.

What do you regret? Can you look to the future instead? Who are you bitter or resentful against? Can you release them and focus on the future instead? If you will, this is God's promise for you:

> Then I will make up to you for the years that the swarming locust has eaten, the creeping locust, the stripping locust and the gnawing locust, My great army which I sent among you. You will have plenty to eat and be satisfied and praise the name of the LORD your God, Who has dealt wondrously with you; then My people will never be put to shame. Thus you will know that I am

in the midst of Israel, and that I am the LORD your God, and there is no other; and My people will never be put to shame. (Joel 2:25–27)

Any regrets can be covered by Jesus' redeeming blood. Any bitterness can be released as we choose to forgive. The worry of regrets and bitterness need not control us. God wants to provide the hope and power we need. Let's make a commitment to refuse to look in the rearview mirror and focus on the drive before us.

Miriam / NUMBERS 12:1–16

Miriam had a lot to worry about. Miriam was the daughter of Jochebed, and she helped her mother put baby Moses into the reed basket. She also went to get her mother when the princess asked for a nurse maid.

As a grown woman she helped Moses lead the Hebrew people with dancing and music, praising God for His marvelous works on their behalf. She was also the person who later criticized Moses' guidance because she was jealous of his new wife, and she thought she should get more credit for her leadership role among the people. As a result of this wrong attitude, Miriam received judgment from God in the form of leprosy, which kept her outside the camp for seven days. She was healed by God because Moses prayed.

I can't help but think that she, along with the other Israelites, pined for the good old days back in Egypt with the leeks and garlic and hard work. Exodus 16:2–3 tells us, "The whole congregation of the sons of Israel grumbled against Moses and Aaron in the wilderness. The sons of Israel said to them, 'Would that we had died by the LORD's hand in the land of Egypt, when we sat by the pots of meat, when we ate bread to the full; for you have brought us out into this wilderness to kill this whole assembly with hunger.'" Oh yes, they had pots of meat and bread in Egypt, but they conveniently forgot about the hard work as slaves. They had turned their regrets into grumbling and complaining.

Could the discontent and regrets of leaving Egypt have fed

Miriam's jealousy toward her brother? Maybe. But whatever the source may have been, Miriam focused on the past and was bitter toward her brother, believing she had not been acknowledged properly for her leadership. She may have thought, *If only God had chosen me to guide, things would be different.* The former joys of worshiping and rejoicing were overshadowed by a woman who looked in the rearview mirror of regret and bitterness.

We don't want to be like Miriam, and we don't have to be.

 ## DISCUSSION QUESTIONS

1. What do you have the most regrets about? Who is the focus of bitterness or resentment in your life?

2. Can you give an example of when you looked in the rearview mirror of regrets or bitterness and some sort of "crash" happened as a result?

3. Read Philippians 3:1–14; 2 Corinthians 11:22–27; and 1 Timothy 1:12–17. Paul had both good and bad things in his past to "forget." He could have had both regrets (about the bad) and pride (about the good) fill him, yet what was more important to him? How does that speak to you?

4. How does it impact you to realize that "forgetting" doesn't mean "not remembering"?

5. When you worry by regretting the past, do you have a sense that somehow you are changing the past? If so, what truth can you tell yourself?

6. Why is it so hard to forgive? What do you fear most will happen if you forgive the person who has hurt you? How can it be helpful to ask yourself, "Is my bitterness or resentment helping me to gain what I need?"

7. What does Ephesians 4:30–32 and Matthew 6:14–15 command you to do? If it's a command, is it conditional upon another per-

son's attitude (like their asking for our forgiveness for hurting us)?

8. Can you share about an experience of peeling away layers of bitterness?

9. Do you find Isaiah 43:25 meaningful for you? If so, in what way?

10. How can "looking forward" help you to refuse to worry?

11. How do you want to claim the promises in Isaiah 43:18–19 and Joel 2:25–27?

12. Read Numbers 12:1–16. Can you identify with anything from Miriam's experience? How does her story give you hope?

Letter from God

My Precious Daughter,

I did give you the ability to remember the past, but it was My intention that it help you remember My work in the past, not the regrets. I didn't create you with the ability to carry a load of regrets and bitterness. It's not healthy for you. It's not My best for you. Won't you release these loads that weigh you down and hinder your trust in Me?

I understand that it's hard to do that, but I want to help you do it because I want you as spiritually and emotionally healthy as possible. And releasing those painful memories through forgiveness is the key. Forgive yourself because I have (if you've asked Me to).

Forgive others, because your bitterness doesn't cause them any pain. I am the faithful judge. I will take whatever action is necessary to bring justice on your behalf. Put them in My capable hands, and

I guarantee that I'll judge appropriately. I can't pledge to you that you'll see the justice, but I assure you there will be justice. Count on it.

My daughter, turn your attention to My faithfulness each time bitterness or regrets try to steal your joy. Trust in Me. Give me the load. You'll feel so much better.

I love you.

Your Heavenly Father

CHAPTER 9

Tornado a-*Comin'*

Finding the Storm Cellar
of God's Power

*T*his California-bred-and-raised woman couldn't believe it! I looked out at the Illinois landscape from my hotel room and couldn't comprehend the power of the storm that was lighting up the night sky. In Southern California we rarely have thunder and lightning storms, much less lightning flashes that light up the sky several times a second. I was fascinated and transfixed looking out the window. The TV blared the warning that a tornado was possible and urged everyone to stay tuned for further coverage.

Should I be looking out the window? Maybe the storm will break the window; the wind seems to be blowing so hard. I knew I needed to get some sleep to be at my best for my speaking engagement the next day, but I couldn't take my eyes off the electrical show outside my window. It was captivating. Even the potential danger couldn't take away my fascination. Confident that the hotel staff would wake up everyone if we needed to take shelter, I fell asleep as the lightning continued to light up the room.

A tornado never did appear that evening, but speaker and writer

Pamela Sonnenmoser told me of the time she lived through the devastation of one.

As I made my way through the winding road leading home, the clouds began to gather green and ominous. The wind blew debris across the road and leaves poured from green trees as if it were an autumn day. Suddenly the shrill shrieks of the emergency broadcast system came on the radio. My mind began to race through the tornado safety tips my husband, John, had taught me when we moved to the Midwest from my home in Southern California.

The announcer on the radio stated in monotones that a tornado with one-hundred-mile-an-hour winds was heading south to Rushville, Missouri, at a rate of thirty-five miles per hour. As I turned into my driveway the monotone voice estimated that we had ten minutes before the tornado would arrive in Rushville. I felt as if I were in a made-for-TV movie.

In our home, I made a few phone calls to warn several people, but I didn't know where John was. My heart raced because the tornado was supposed to cross John's path as he returned home from work. *What if something happens to him?* I couldn't bear the thought. All I knew for sure was that I had to get to the cellar.

When I opened the front door, fear came blasting through with debris and wind and rain. I knew I couldn't make it to the cellar door. Slamming my body against the door, I shut it against the storm. I didn't know what to do. Remembering more tornado tips, I ran to the center of our house and surrounded my body with the blankets from my bed. A nearby laundry basket would have to serve as protection for my head. There was nothing I could do except pray as the roaring sound of the nearby tornado was accented by sounds of breaking glass and tearing metal. *When will this terror stop? Why didn't I go to the cellar as soon as the emergency system sounded? John is going to be angry with me. O God, protect me!*

After a few minutes that seemed like hours I emerged from my blanket cocoon and went outside. My legs gave way and I kneeled sobbing as I saw the flattened cellar house completely covered by the cedar tree that had stood next to it for years. God had protected me from the storm. He knew my "storm cellar" wouldn't be safe so He provided His own place of protection. I should have been in that pile of rubble, buried and trapped, waiting for someone to find me cowering in a corner. But I wasn't. I was fine, and all of the destruction was temporary. *But where is John?* I sobbed.

Soon John's car headed up the long driveway. I ran out to greet him, and as he hugged me, I leaned on him and cried tears of fear, relief, and joy. Then he told me that a tire blowout had prevented him from crossing the path of the tornado.

Pamela concluded her story by saying,

We don't have to live in worry. We just need to walk in faith and trust that God is in control even when we can't see what He is doing. I firmly believe that God protected us the day of the tornado. Even though logic said I should go to the cellar and John was frustrated when his tire blew, God was using those things to keep us safe. There was no reason for worry, fear, or frustration.

Pamela's story reminds us that we don't need to worry, because God is powerful enough to take care of us, according to His will. Whenever I start to worry, I think of four principles about His power that will protect us when the tornados of life come roaring at us:

- God can do *whatever* He wants, He's experienced;
- God can do *all* He wants, He's extravagant;
- God can do *however* He wants, He's exacting;
- God can do *whenever* He wants, He's expeditious.

God Can Do Whatever He Wants, He's Experienced

God is an expert! God knows the "what" that He desires to accomplish. The "what" is the result of His plan. But as we're heading toward the "what," we get worried. We wonder if God really is capable and powerful enough to handle our situation as the tornado of problems heads for us. Sometimes I do wonder if God is standing in heaven wringing His hands, muttering, "Oh no, I really hadn't banked on this happening! What in the world should I do about this?"

NOT! God knows the result He has in mind, and nothing will stop Him. That is what the miracle of the feeding of the five thousand in John chapter 6 teaches us. "Therefore Jesus, lifting up His eyes and seeing that a large crowd was coming to Him, said to Philip, 'Where are we to buy bread, so that these may eat?' This He was saying to test him, *for He Himself knew what He was intending to do*" (John 6:5–6, italics mine).

Jesus knew all along what He was going to do, but He wanted to include His disciples in the miracle. Can't you just envision the disciples' concern and worry when Jesus asked that question? Philip must have been thinking, *Oh my! If* you *don't know how to feed them, I sure don't. Why are you asking* me? *I don't want the responsibility!*

That's sometimes how you and I feel when God is in the process of bringing us to the "what" of His plan. We're wondering what's going on. And we begin to doubt God's power to take care of the problem or situation. *But God knows what He intends to do!*

Charles Swindoll encourages us by writing, "*When you face an impossibility, leave it in the hands of the Specialist.* Refuse to calculate. Refuse to doubt. Refuse to work it out by yourself. Refuse to worry or encourage others to worry."[1]

Darlene Grimes learned that lesson early in life. She had been taking care of herself since age fourteen because her mother was mentally ill and her father had left them many years earlier. Darlene learned that only God could help her as her mother repeatedly kicked her out of the house—her mother's one-bedroom apartment in Brooklyn, New York.

She explains, "I had begun taking care of my mother when I was eleven, doing the household chores and cashing the welfare check to buy groceries. With my grandmother's encouragement, I learned to look to God to provide for everything."

When Darlene was sixteen, her mother kicked her out again because her mom was planning to marry her husband's best friend. Breaking down, Darlene remembers screaming at God, "Why me? When will this stop? Why can't I enjoy my childhood like my friends? Why are you allowing this to happen?"

Then she got a revelation. "I could kill myself, go to heaven, and forget all this." But in that moment she heard God say, "You don't want to do that, Darlene! When people kill themselves they rob themselves of the future I have planned for them on this earth."

"Okay," Darlene argued, "then you will have to find me a place to live that I can afford." She fell asleep, exhausted, yet with confidence that God had heard her plea and would provide a solution.

The next morning Darlene went to the school counselor's office feeling heavy-hearted but still looking for her miracle. She told the school counselor about her dilemma, and he replied, "I'm going on a sabbatical to Europe for the next school year, and I'm leaving next month. Will you live in my home, feed my dog and cats, and watch over the place for me?"

Darlene says,

> So there I was, less than twelve hours later, with a golden solution to my homeless problem. My own place, right by the subway. And living above me was another teacher from my school to whom I could go if I had an emergency. It was perfect! Better than I could have imagined.
>
> From that point on, I have refused to worry. I give my problems to God, who always takes care of them. Not always in ways I may approve of, but always, in looking back with 20/20 hindsight, the perfect solution for that time. As I continued to listen to God, cast my cares upon Him, and talk to Him daily, I graduated cum laude (at twenty-one years of age) from a private university on a full scholarship, grateful that I listened to God that night when I thought the only solution was to kill myself.

God showed Darlene His awesome power, and God wants us to trust that same power for whatever problem we are facing. Let's make Jeremiah 32:17 our watchword when worry threatens us like a tornado: "'Ah Lord GOD! Behold, You have made the heavens and the earth by Your great power and by Your outstretched arm! Nothing is too difficult for You.'"

Nothing! Absolutely nothing is too difficult for God. He can do *whatever* He wants, because He's *experienced*! Charles Swindoll explains,

> It's difficult to reconstruct in the English language the full color and impact of the Hebrew words used in this verse. The best we can do is to say, "No, absolutely nothing for You is extraordinary or surpassing." The text begins with the strongest negative known to the Hebrew language. "No, nothing, absolutely nothing for You, Lord, is extraordinary." What a statement to ponder![2]

The next time worry starts eating at you, tell yourself, "God knows exactly what He intends to do. Nothing is too big for Him to handle."

God Can Do All He Wants, He's Extravagant

God isn't interested only in the result; He's interested in the "extent" of what He does. There's no limit to all that God can do. Paul wrote in his letter to the Philippians, "And my God will supply all your needs according to His riches in glory in Christ Jesus" (Philippians 4:19). The word *supply* is a Greek word for "fill." Paul didn't write "some of your needs" or "most of your needs," but "all of your needs." God is saying "Fill 'er up!"

My friend and fellow writer Gayle DeSalles has seen the truth of God's extravagance. Now, I suspect you're thinking that I'm going to continue writing something about Gayle, like, God has provided her with a magnificent mansion, a million-dollar paycheck, and three cars! But that's not Gayle's story of God's extravagance.

Actually, Gayle has been out of work for eight months. Led by God, she moved to look for a new job. Even though she has worked part-time for a friend, God hasn't provided that new job yet. She wrote me,

> I'm well, but still have not found permanent work. I never in a million years dreamed it would be this tough. As you might expect, I could share a few stories of fear; yes, worry, but also God's provision and care. Most of all, I think I'm learning lots about God. I've incurred some debt, how could I not? But no creditors are mad at me. All my bills are being paid on time. Haven't won any lottery, but God has made provision in little ways and a few not-so-little ways. I have cried a few tears a few times, like last week when I almost had a job but then someone else was selected. I am not lying when I say that all is well with my soul.

Gayle's story is more about God's ability to do all He wants than what we usually think of as a "success story." God is providing for all her needs without a job, our usual means of support in providing for our needs. He's not providing all her wants, but He *is* being faithful in what really matters. Will Gayle get a job in time? Yes, I'm sure she will. But what is more important is the "all" that God is doing in her *heart* as she draws closer to Him.

As Gayle knows, God doesn't always wrap up everything in our lives in a neat package. Our definition of *all* is often not the same as God's. Just ask Alice King Greenwood, whose teenage grandson, Chris, is tall and strong but mentally dysfunctional. Even with medication, he needs constant supervision because of irrational behavior. She shared the following story in an e-mail to me.

One night concern and worry about Chris' future kept Alice awake. Her grandmother's heart was breaking, "O God!" she cried out, "What will become of Chris? I see no way out of this impossible situation. Please heal him!" Alice was overwhelmed with the immensity of the problem and her utter helplessness to solve it.

As God seemed to whisper, "Trust me," she recalled a childhood experience in which she learned the real meaning of trust. Alice had climbed up on the cross-boards of the fence near the family barn. Then her bare toes pushed their way into between-board spaces in the barn wall. Up she climbed until she reached the high windowsill. From there her legs gripped the overhang of the roof and over the edge she scooted.

She was playing on top of the barn while her father milked the cow and finished his evening chores. He called out to Alice, "Come down now. It's time to go back to the house."

Alice scooted to the edge of the roof and stared at the ground below. She tried sitting on the edge of the roof and stretching her legs as far as they would go, but she still could not reach the windowsill. Her bare feet could not find the toeholds in the wall, and the fence looked far, far away.

Terrified, she began to cry, "I can't get down. It's too far."

Her dad set down his bucket and lifted up his long, strong arms. "Just jump," he answered, "I'll catch you." Although he pleaded with her for several minutes, Alice could not bring herself to take that long leap. Finally, he sadly walked away, saying, "Then you'll have to get down the best way you can."

Alice lay down on her stomach and scooted backward over the edge, intending to drop safely and softly to the ground. Shaking all over, she pushed herself little by little, letting her legs hang over the side as far as they could. Her hands tightly gripped the roof overhang, but suddenly she lost her grip. Down she came, flopping this way and that, until she landed in a little heap on the ground. Picking herself up and not finding anything really wrong, she went into the house. But she regretted that she hadn't put her trust in her father.

As Alice remembered that incident she could sense her heavenly Father stretching out His strong arms and pleading with her to let Him handle Chris's situation. She realized,

> Chris will be in good hands. His handicap is no surprise to God. He knew Chris even while his body was being formed in his mother's womb. God already has made plans for Chris, and I can trust Him to carry out those plans. Since that night, God has not miraculously healed my grandson. Chris may remain mentally impaired as long as he's on this earth, if God so wills. But I know I can completely trust God to accomplish His purpose in Chris's life.

God doesn't always solve our problems with the "all" we'd like. But He always does *all that He wants* in the midst of the tornado because He's an extravagant God. He provides and protects much more than we could ever deserve.

Ephesians 3:20–21 speaks of God's amazing provision: "Now to Him who is able to do far more abundantly beyond all that we ask or think, according to the power that works within us, to Him be the glory. . . ."

When worry flings itself at you, feeling like a tornado's fierce winds whipping around you, hold onto this truth: God can do *all* He wants; He's extravagant. He's extravagantly in love with you and wants only the best for you. He may not answer all your prayers in the way you desire, and He may not reveal His power in the ways that you believe you need, but He does promise to do all for you that is in your best interests.

God Can Do However He Wants, He's Exacting

We've talked about the *result* of God's power, and the *extent* of His power, but God is also involved in His own unique *method* for taking care of the very thing we're worried about. And *unique* is the operative word. We cannot possibly see everything that God sees from His vantage point. His knowledge is greater than we could ever comprehend. He is working supernaturally in and through everything. And His methods are often different (and sometimes opposed) to the way that we would solve our worries.

Isaiah 55:8–9 tells us, "'For My thoughts are not your thoughts, nor are your ways My ways,' declares the LORD. 'For as the heavens are higher than the earth, so are My ways higher than your ways and My thoughts than your thoughts.'"

As the winds blow from the tornado, are you looking for God to take care of your worry in a particular way? Are you thinking there's only *one* way for your problem to be solved? Remember, God is both creative and exacting; He knows exactly what He intends to do, and He often shows His power in the most amazing ways.

My friend and former neighbor Estella Olin reminded me of the creative way God got her attention back when we were living on the same street. She had recently received Christ as her Savior and, as she attended our neighborhood ladies Bible study, began to grow in her faith and trust in God.

Then the world came crashing in as her husband unexpectedly divorced her. She was terrified.

> I couldn't believe God had allowed this horrible thing to happen to me and my family. I loved God and had dedicated myself to follow His Word. Now instead of reaping good things, my whole world was being ripped apart. How could He be in charge, when I could only see my own pain and worry? I had lost my husband, my helpmate, my children's father, and I was in peril of losing my faith in God.
>
> I called out to God, begging Him to heal my marriage. But His answer was no. *How would I survive?* I had three daughters and an infant son. I didn't work. I couldn't understand why God would turn His back on me, and I began to cry out to Him. "Your Word says you won't give me a trial I can't endure or escape, and yet I feel so alone and I see no escape."
>
> I felt bitterness enter my life. This was the first trial I had to endure as a baby Christian, and it was inconceivable to me that

something like this could happen to a believer. I worried about my future and my children's. I felt like Job, and read that book of the Bible, hoping God would show me why He allowed bad things to happen to His people. I waited for God to answer me, and I heard nothing. It made me feel as though I had believed in vain.

One day, in a fit of worry and anger, I noticed afresh the plaque that I'd put on the wall when I became a Christian. It was Romans 8:28 (NKJV): "All things work together for good to those who love God." Those words mocked me. That verse was a lie! I jerked the plaque off the wall and threw it into the trash.

A few days later I walked past the wall where the plaque had been hanging, and it was hanging there again! I couldn't believe it. I don't know who put it up there, but in that moment I realized God had heard my prayers. He wanted me to believe His Word without knowing the how or the reason. He had uniquely given me His message; Romans 8:28 really was true. He reminded me what Job had said, "Though He slay me, yet will I trust Him" (Job 13:15 NKJV). I decided that would be my commitment also. I released the problem of my future and said, "If God chooses to have me go through this, then He'll use it for my good according to His will."

Estella concludes, "I am not going to tell you that from that moment on my trial was over. Far from it. It took a long time for the unique work God started in my life to come to completion. I find that when I am in the midst of a trial, I remember how God perfectly and in His time met my needs."

Today Estella is happily married to her second husband, and her children are grown and following God. At the time Estella didn't like the method God was using. And that's usually the case. Our eyes are blinded to God's purposes. We think that everything should go perfectly. But God can work however He wants to overcome our worry.

What are you worried about? Does it seem like God isn't answering your prayers with a reasonable solution? Does it seem like the tornado is crushing you? Refocus on God's power. He is exacting in His methods. He knows the plans He has for the pressure you're feeling, the job that won't come, or the illness that won't heal. He can do *however* He wants! Look for it!

God Can Do Whenever He Wants, He's Expeditious

We've heard it a lot. Timing is everything. And everything to worry about! We hear and experience so much pressure about time: Don't waste it; use every moment wisely; you'll only go by this way once. And then we start worrying when God doesn't keep His end of the bargain about time. He delays. He's on His own time schedule.

Time! What a worrisome gift from God. We need to learn to trust God about our own management of time, and then we must also trust God for His timing in our lives.

When I think about managing my own time with God's help I can look back and remember the exact principle that helped me release and worry less about my time pressures. Someone shared with me, "God will give me enough time to do what He wants me to do."

Psalm 127:1–2 says, "Unless the LORD builds the house, they labor in vain who build it; unless the LORD guards the city, the watchman keeps awake in vain. It is vain for you to rise up early, to retire late, to eat the bread of painful labors; for He gives to His beloved even in his sleep."

I began to believe that God could determine what I should get done in a day. Normally I would think I had to check off every item on my to-do list in order to be a super Christian. But then I began saying, "Okay, Lord, what do you want me to put first on my list?" and "What do you want me to do next?" I began to relax. "If I don't get everything done, then that's okay. I will finish what God wants me to complete because He is directing me."

Mary Beth Nelson has learned the same thing. She told me,

> I am mindful of a day last summer when I studied a list of eleven activities that I thought must be accomplished before the day ended. I suddenly became overwhelmed with frustration. I thought, *It's impossible for me to complete all of this today, and I should!*
>
> But then I remembered that I'm not supposed to be anxious about *anything* (Philippians 4:6). I reconsidered my list. Surely some of the activities were not immediate. It might just be a matter of setting priorities. After revising the items, only four of the eleven proved necessary. The other seven remained on the list

with less importance. Changing the impossibility to a comfortable possibility, I happily began my morning's work, concentrating on item number one, knowing that I could take more time to do it well. After accomplishing it, I began the second.

At the end of the day I smiled as I reviewed the items. I had completed the top six, two more than absolutely necessary. I felt relaxed. God is helping me realize that overloaded expectations result in disappointment, worry, and frustration. Taking a step at a time allows a more joyful attitude and actions that are pleasing to Him.

God can act *whenever* He wants in the midst of our time pressures. He's expeditious in directing our way if we will just turn it over to Him. At the beginning of each day, write out your list and ask God what He wants you to do item by item, project by project. He's a wonderful time manager! He's expeditious—speedy to get done what He wants done.

But the bigger challenge is trusting God when He delays in fulfilling His plan—at least from our perspective. We worry because He's not coming through for us. Where is His power? Why is He waiting? We fear the tornado is going to blow everything away.

Where Are You, Lord?

Just ask Lori Scott. Her husband's job opening in another city required them to move, and their house wasn't selling. She tells me what happened via an e-mail.

"I really wanted to trust God to work things out, but 'What ifs?' ran through my mind like restless hounds. I slept fitfully. I snapped at my children for no reason. I got teary-eyed around friends. I ate entire jars of pickles in a single day. I hovered near the phone, waiting for the Realtor to call. I despaired whenever I spotted a SOLD sign someplace else in the city."

Lori and her husband knew their home was a "tough sell." Before they purchased it, it had sat on the market for two years, switching real-estate agencies twice. It had very little backyard space. To make matters worse, two comparable houses went on the market with similar asking prices. Both stood within a half-mile of Lori's house and had approximately the same square footage of living space and large well-kept yards.

One month passed. Anxiety seized Lori each time she marked off another calendar day. Her pickle supply dwindled. Knowing she needed relief from the worry that gnawed at her heart, Lori sought comfort by reading through her favorite book of the Bible, Isaiah.

While out on a walk Lori saw one of the competing neighborhood houses with a "SOLD" sign. She says, "For a moment I couldn't breathe. Didn't God *know* we were running out of time? Or was He going to wait until the last minute before relieving my trouble in order to stretch my faith to the limit?"

Reaching home, she pulled out her Bible and opened it to where she'd left off. At first she couldn't concentrate, so she laid out her feelings before God. "Lord," Lori prayed, "I know you often answer prayers in dramatic, sometimes last-minute ways, so that we learn to depend on you. But I'm having a hard time waiting. I just want you to know that if we sold our house early, before we absolutely had to, I'd still see Your hand in it. I'd still know you made it happen."

With a sigh, she opened her eyes and started reading. Then Isaiah 52:12 hit her fretful heart: "But you will not leave in haste or go in flight; for the Lord will go before you, the God of Israel will be your rear guard" (NIV).

She says, "I sat back, stunned. I'm not used to God answering so quickly and plainly, but there was the answer to my frank plea. He was telling me, 'Hey! I'm God, remember? I've prepared the way to the new job. If I can make a clear path there, I can tie up the loose ends here. You can trust me as the rear guard.' Then I realized I had put my confidence not in God but in myself. Since I had little control of the situation, worry was my master."

Bowing her head, Lori immediately surrendered her anxieties to God's care. She explained, "It's hard to describe, but when I relinquished control, those fears evaporated like morning dew and were replaced with eager anticipation. I felt with certainty that the house would sell. And I could wait."

That very night Lori and her husband got an offer on their house, which they accepted. Lori says, "Now when I begin to tense up, I try to remember the lesson God so eloquently laid out before me. It's a lesson of trust, of seeking reassurance in God's Word, and of surrendering fears to God."

Lori isn't alone in waiting upon God. It's a popular topic in the Bible, and there is almost no worse situation than waiting when your own reputation is being ruined and God doesn't seem to be doing anything about it. The psalmist must have felt that as he wrote, "Rest in the LORD and wait patiently for Him; do not fret because of him who prospers in his way, because of the man who carries out wicked schemes. Cease from anger and forsake wrath; do not fret; it leads only to evildoing" (Psalm 37:7–8).

Vindication!

Bev Hamel was concerned about her reputation at work, and Psalm 37 became her key to stop worrying. She was called into her boss's office and told she could be fired or choose to quit. A week before, it was discovered that a lot of money was missing from the security office safe, which was her responsibility. With a heavily burdened mind, knowing she was innocent, she signed the form to quit and then went into the office of her supervisor, who was also a Christian. They wept together for an hour, both knowing she had been framed by a disgruntled fellow employee.

Bev shared with me,

> The days that followed were a mix of anger and panic. I was fearful that my Christian reputation was blown. Later the anxiety grew when job interviews fizzled. I feared that the company had blackballed me from getting other work.
>
> Then one morning, in my time with the Lord, I ran into Psalm 37. Right away I was admonished not to fret over the situation (v. 1). But as I went through the psalm, I counted the phrase *fret not* three, yes, three times. How could I fret when verse by verse, the promises in Psalm 37 exploded in my heart? I would dwell and be fed (v. 3); He would give me the desires of my heart (v. 4); He would make my right standing go ahead of me (v. 19); I would live secure (v. 27); and I wouldn't be left in the hand of the enemy or be condemned (v. 33). Me, fret? NEVER!

God provided another good job for Bev in His timing. And she gave me this update: "One day, while I visited the old workplace, I asked where my accuser was and learned that two months after the incident she had suddenly left. Psalm 37:10 (NIV) was fulfilled; 'Though you look for them, they will not be found.'"

Bev resisted worry, and God provided for both her job and her reputation. Her trust in God has soared to a new level.

If you are experiencing God's delay in responding to your pleas about your concerns and worries, take heart. God does take His time, but He controls time and doesn't need to be in a hurry. He is never late. You can trust Him. God can act *whenever* He wants because He's expeditious.

The next time you feel like a tornado of worries is heading your way, trust God. He is our storm cellar of protection and care. He can do whatever, all, however, and whenever He wants. We can trust Him.

Esther / Book of ESTHER

Esther had a lot to worry about. She stood outside the king's chamber and realized that within a few minutes she could be dead. That didn't happen, of course. Her story is about how God used a young Jewish girl, who became Queen of Persia and Media, to protect the Jewish people from extermination. And there's no more potent story in the Bible about God's power than the book of Esther. The amazing thing is that God's name and His power is never mentioned, yet His fingerprints are all over this book.

Here are just some of the ways that God's power is shown in Esther's story:

- Queen Vashti refuses to obey the King and she is displaced.
- The king is encouraged to find a new wife through a beauty contest.
- Mordecai sends his cousin, Esther, to the contest.
- Esther finds favor with the person in charge of the beauty contestants.
- The king chooses Esther as his new queen.

- Mordecai stops an assassination plot against the king, but the king doesn't reward him.
- The enemy of the Jews, Haman, plots to have the Jews exterminated.
- Esther finds favor with the king to come unannounced into his presence.
- The king has insomnia and reads the book of records, "just happening" to turn to the page with the details of Mordecai reporting the plot, and realizes Mordecai was not rewarded.
- Haman appears at that very moment and is sent to give honor (the king's reward) to Haman's enemy, Mordecai.
- Esther plans two banquets and is seemingly attacked by Haman in front of the king.
- The king commands Haman's death and gives Esther permission to have the Jews protect themselves when the citizens attack them.

Talk about espionage and suspense! God's power is evident in so many ways. There were many things that Esther could have worried about. And of course the most famous line that shows her victory over worry is "Go, assemble all the Jews who are found in Susa, and fast for me; do not eat or drink for three days, night or day. I and my maidens also will fast in the same way. And thus I will go in to the king, which is not according to the law; and if I perish, I perish" (Esther 4:16).

Esther submitted herself to God's protection and care. We want to be just like Esther, and we can be!

 DISCUSSION QUESTIONS

1. What is the most serious weather you have ever been in? How did you feel at that time? In what ways were you worried, and how did you handle it?

2. Reread the story of Jesus' miracle in John chapter 6 and see if you can pick out any new insights about worry. Can you share a story

of when you conquered fear because you realized that God "knew what He was intending to do" (John 6:6)?

3. Read Jeremiah 32:17 again. Jeremiah expresses how powerful God is by making a contrast. What is it? How does it speak to you? Can you think of another way to say "nothing" that would be even more meaningful to you?

4. When you think of the word *extravagant,* what do you think of? What other words could be used? How have you seen God's extravagance revealed in your life?

5. Philippians 4:19 gives a wonderful promise. How have you seen its truth revealed in your life previously? Is it hard or easy to believe the "all" of that verse?

6. When God doesn't provide everything we'd like, do you think that means He hasn't kept His promise of Philippians 4:19? Explain your answer.

7. What do you currently need Ephesians 3:17–20 to give you peace about?

8. Read Isaiah 55:8–9. How do those verses explain God's workings (especially when He does things differently than you think He should)? Can you share a time when God worked differently than you expected, and then you could see His hand in the situation?

9. Think about Psalm 127:1–2 and the statement "God will give me enough time to do what He wants me to do." How do the statement and the Scripture help you to worry less about your time pressures?

10. Read Psalm 37. Which verse is most meaningful to you in whatever worry you are facing?

11. Scan the book of Esther. Which "fingerprint" of God is most meaningful to you?

12. Which of these points is most important to you?

   • God can do whatever He wants, He's experienced.

- God can do all He wants, He's extravagant.
- God can do however He wants, He's exacting.
- God can do whenever He wants, He's expeditious.

Letter from God

My Precious Daughter,

I am powerful. Nothing makes Me worried. Nothing surprises Me. I know exactly what I'm planning. Though your thinking is limited, Mine is not. I can see everything, and I know everything. Trust Me and My intentions for your good.

Nothing is too hard for Me! I know exactly all that I'm planning. I never stop midway. I fulfill all My plan. Know that I never stop before I'm finished.

Nothing is confusing to Me. I know exactly how I'm going to work. I have multiple choices, and I know the best way. You can believe I'll use whatever method is best.

Nothing rushes Me. I know exactly the timing for what I have planned. I know it's hard to wait, but waiting will build your faith and trust in Me. I don't make you wait without a reason. Trust that I am in control of all the details.

Beloved, I can do anything. And everything I do in your life is meant to draw you closer to My loving heart. Draw close to Me. Rest in Me! My arms are open to you and I'm working on your behalf.

I love you.

Your Heavenly Father

EPILOGUE

Windy Day

Having the Spirit Flow in Your Life

I woke up at five in the morning and immediately recognized the sound of the wind whipping the trees outside our bedroom window. For a moment I wanted to roll back over and forget about my run. *Oh well, I won't be able to get back to sleep anyway,* I thought, *and even if I walk the whole way it'll be something.* Pushing against the wind usually made me a discouraged runner, but at least I'd get some exercise.

A little while later I headed out and found the wind wasn't that formidable. I began an easy jog, and the breeze wasn't a bother at all. When I headed back home, downwind, it pushed me along. *Hey, that was a great run!* I ended up thinking.

As I thought of the wind I realized that wind is referred to in the Bible in many ways, but for our theme of worry we can look at two significant ways it is discussed. The first one is in James 1:5–8; the brother of Jesus wrote,

> But if any of you lacks wisdom, let him ask of God, who gives to all generously and without reproach, and it will be given to him. But he must ask in faith without any doubting, for the one who doubts is like the surf of the sea driven and tossed by the wind. For that man ought not to expect that he will receive anything from the Lord, being a double-minded man, unstable in all his ways.

Worry is like that kind of wind. It tosses us about in our emotions, reactions, and decisions. It makes us spiritually seasick. But I hope that by finishing this book, you have felt more land-solid, better able to trust God with your fears.

We started out in the Prologue discovering the differences about fear, thought, and worry. As you recall that information in the future, don't cover over your worry by using other, more "acceptable," words. Instead, face it and deal with it, in God's power, by calling upon Him.

Our first chapter stresses how our greatest fear could become our greatest blessing, because God has a plan. And remember, most of the things we worry about never come true. We need to call worry what it is: sin! We're not trusting God when we're worrying.

The second chapter encourages us to fight worry by meditating on how much God loves you and me. He wants the *very best* for us, and everything He chooses for us is for our good! His love is pure, perfect, and prudent. He can never want anything that is bad for us. That's definitely something to meditate upon when worry assails us.

Prayer is the focus of the third chapter. That's what we all should think of at the very first hint of worry. It works! By the way, have you made your "peace card" yet? If not, please do it right now. I guarantee it's going to help you!

The fourth chapter reminds us that gratitude protects our heart from worry. When we think negatively, everything gets blown out of proportion. But keeping a positive spirit helps us thank God for everything, and this attitude drives worry away.

One of the primary ways I find the strength to fight worry is the subject of our fifth chapter: God's sovereignty. When we believe our mighty and wise Lord God of the universe is completely in charge and capable of being in control of everything that happens in our lives, then we have confidence to tell worry to "buzz off!"

Another way we'll say "leave me alone" to worry is covered in chapter 6: believing that God knows how He wants us to grow and change through the troubles we face. By seeing the good that comes, if what we're worried about really does come true, we cannot be held hostage by our fears.

In chapter 7 we find that worry often causes us to try to control others, but it doesn't work! Worry about others, even couched in "love and concern," is refusing to believe that God can work in other people's lives much more effectively than we can!

Most people don't think of the subject of chapter 8 as worry, but regrets and bitterness are indeed based in worry. We're just worrying about the past rather than the future. But we can negate their power over us by forgiving ourselves and others.

Chapter 9 focuses on God's power, and that powerful truth reminds us that God can do whatever, all, however, and whenever He wants! And His work is always intended for our good and His glory.

As you read this book you may have wondered about your relationship with God. And that's the second way the word *wind* is used in Scripture. Jesus said, "'The wind blows where it wishes and you hear the sound of it, but do not know where it comes from and where it is going; so is everyone who is born of the Spirit'" (John 3:8).

If you've recognized that you haven't experienced a "rebirth," a spiritual birth by which you enter the kingdom of God, then you can ask Jesus to become your Lord and Savior right now. Invite Him into your heart and life by praying a prayer something like this:

Heavenly Father, thank you for sending Jesus to die on the cross in my place. I recognize that I need a Savior because I have sinned and I can never be good enough to earn my way into heaven. I ask you to come into my life and become my Savior, my Lord, and my Master. Thank you for forgiving all my sins and making me a new creature in Christ. Amen.

If you prayed that prayer, please let someone know who can encourage you to grow in your new walk with Christ. Although being a Christian doesn't mean we'll never worry, with the wind of the Holy Spirit "blowing" within us, we do have the power to diminish worry's hold over us.

Dear reader, I'd love to hear from you. You can reach me at: *Kathy@KathyCollardMiller.com.*

SUGGESTIONS FOR GROUP LEADERS

𝒯hank you for being willing to take on the challenge of leading a group of women through the discussion questions in this book. I know what a joy it's going to be, because I have led many groups through various studies, and it's always a treat to see what God does in each woman. Here are some ideas that I hope will make your time more meaningful.

Don't be afraid.

If this is your first attempt at doing something like this, I applaud you! God has called you to this role, so you can be confident that He will guide and empower you for the task. Remember, it's not about you—it's about Him. Though we are all inadequate in ourselves, He will give us success because He will be glorified through it. He will show up! Even if you make mistakes, be assured that He'll use you anyway. And if you make obvious mistakes, just ask the group to forgive you and ask for their help in correcting any difficulty you're having.

Don't talk more than the other women.

This is not a preaching assignment; this is a "guiding" assignment. You are not supposed to "teach" these discussion questions; you are guiding the women through the questions with the intention of drawing out what God wants to do within them.

Don't try to give the impression that you are perfect or don't have your own problems.

Share your own struggles and problems concisely. KISS: Keep it short and simple!

Don't try to solve the women's problems.

This is a "no rescuing zone." If someone shares a problem, don't spend a lot of time giving her solutions. Otherwise the group becomes a counseling session. If someone needs more concrete help, say something like, "I'd love to give you some practical ideas to consider. I'll call you tomorrow (or whenever you can)." Encourage other women to contact the woman directly, outside of the group, so that you don't take too much time during the meeting.

Let the group choose how they want to share their answers.

Let the group choose whether being able to share the answers to the questions verbally is dependent upon having written out the answers ahead of time. Some groups require this, and some don't.

If you have the time, call each member of the group during the week.

Don't feel pressured about this but, depending upon your time, consider calling one or more members during the week.

Remember, there's no "wrong" answer.

Unless someone gives a theologically incorrect answer that could point other members in a wrong direction spiritually, just say, "Thanks for sharing that."

Try to get everyone to participate.

Don't let one or two people monopolize the group. Say something like, "Let's hear from someone who hasn't shared yet today." Feel free to call on someone in particular unless you sense that they are totally uncomfortable with speaking out.

You'll notice that my goal in these Discussion Questions is not just to have the facts and information about the Scriptures revealed, but to offer thought-provoking questions on how the Bible can relate to and be applied to practical life. Focus more on that aspect of your time together, and I believe there will be more heart-change within the women in your group.

Be *encouraged*!

God has called and chosen you for an incredible and privileged assignment.

Endnotes

PROLOGUE *Dense Fog Predicted*
1. Dr. Archibald Hart, *The Anxiety Cure* (Nashville: Word Publishing, 1999), 5.
2. Ibid., 156–157.

CHAPTER ONE *Anticipating a Storm*
1. From Matthew Henry's Unabridged Commentary, available on Bible Explorer, Copyright 1999, Epiphany Software.
2. Spiros Zodhiates, *The Complete Word Study Dictionary, New Testament* (Chattanooga, Tenn.: AMG Publishers, 1992), 1341.
3. Ibid., 63.
4. W. E. Vine, *Vine's Expository Dictionary* (Old Tappan, N.J.: Revell, 1981), 163.
5. Edith Deen, *All the Women of the Bible* (New York: HarperSan-Francisco, 1983), 51.

CHAPTER TWO *Walking on the Sunny Side*
1. Kathy Collard Miller, *Why Do I Put So Much Pressure on Myself and Others?* (Longwood, Fla.: Xulon Press, 2003), 13.
2. Victoria Neufeldt, Editor-in-Chief, *Webster's New World Dictionary,* Third College edition (New York: Prentice Hall, 1988), 1084.
3. Summarized from Verda Glick, *Deliver the Ransom Alone* (Harrisonburg, Va.: Christian Light Publications, 1999).

CHAPTER THREE *Catching* the *Rainbow*

1. Shari Prange, "Forum Column," *National Geographic*, December 2001.

CHAPTER FOUR *Don't Forget* Your *Umbrella*

1. Charles Swindoll, *Questions Christians Ask, Bible Study Guide* (Fullerton, Calif.: Insight for Living, n.d.), 24.
2. Charles Swindoll, *Laugh Again, Bible Study Guide* (Fullerton, Calif.: Insight for Living, n.d.), 101.
3. Dr. Archibald Hart, *The Anxiety Cure* (Nashville: Word Publishing, 1999); Dr. William Backus, *The Good News About Worry* (Minneapolis, Minn.: Bethany House Publishers, 1991).
4. Rick Warren, *The Purpose-Driven Life* (Grand Rapids, Mich.: Zondervan, 2002), 90.

CHAPTER FIVE *Seeing Past* the *Snowstorm*

1. Charles Swindoll, *Stones of Remembrance, Bible Study Guide* (Anaheim, Calif.: Insight for Living, 1988), 5.
2. Jerry Bridges, *The Practice of Godliness* (Colorado Springs: NavPress, 1996), 158.
3. Joyce Meyer, *Be Anxious for Nothing* (Tulsa, Okla: Harrison House, 1998), 121.
4. Rick Joyner, *50 Days for a Soaring Vision* (Charlotte, N.C.: Morning Star Publications, 2001), 91.

CHAPTER SIX *April Showers* Bring *May Flowers*

1. Kari West, *Dare to Trust, Dare to Hope Again* (Colorado Springs: Cook Communications Ministries, 2001), 126–127.
2. Dr. William Backus, *The Good News About Worry* (Minneapolis, Minn.: Bethany House Publishers, 1991), 167.
3. Dr. Archibald Hart, *The Anxiety Cure* (Nashville: Word Publishing, 1999), 65–66 (adapted).
4. Kitty Chappell, *Sins of a Father: Forgiving the Unforgivable* (Birmingham, Ala.: New Hope Publishers, 2004), 204–207. Used with permission.
5. Janet Holm McHenry, *Daily PrayerWalk* (Colorado Springs: WaterBrook, 2002), 99.
6. Charles Swindoll, *James: Practical and Authentic Living, Bible Study*

Guide (Fullerton, Calif.: Insight for Living, 1980), 17.

7. Ibid., 18.

8. Rick Warren, *The Purpose-Driven Life* (Grand Rapids, Mich.: Zondervan, 2002), 199.

CHAPTER SEVEN *Ice Storm*

1. Found on Myasthenic Meeting Place Web site, *myasthenicmeeting place@listserv.millersville.edu*. January 13, 2004.

2. Neil Anderson, *The Bondage Breaker* (Eugene, Ore.: Harvest House, n.d.).

CHAPTER EIGHT *Rain Behind You*

1. Warren Wiersbe, *Be Joyful* (Wheaton, Ill.: Victor Books, 1974), 98.

2. Beth Moore, *Breaking Free* (Nashville: Broadman & Holman Publishers, 2000), 101.

3. Rick Warren, *The Purpose-Driven Life* (Grand Rapids, Mich.: Zondervan, 2002), 28–29.

4. Tony Beckett and Woodrow Kroll, *Faith Walk,* Devotional, June 27, 2004, *www.backtothebible.org/devotions/features/faithwalk/177*.

5. Dr. Paul Faulkner, *Making Things Right When Things Go Wrong* (West Monroe, La.: Howard Publishing, 1996), 111.

CHAPTER NINE *Tornado a-Comin'*

1. Charles Swindoll, *Three Steps Forward, Two Steps Back* (Nashville: Thomas Nelson Publishers, 1980), 70.

2. Ibid., 62.

About the Author

KATHY COLLARD MILLER is best known for her practical Bible teaching that is marked by vulnerable sharing, humor, and motivation. She speaks thirty to forty times a year, and has shared her messages in thirty states and five foreign countries. Kathy is the bestselling author of forty-eight books, including:

- *When Counting to Ten Isn't Enough*
- *Princess to Princess*
- *Why Do I Put So Much Pressure on Myself and Others?*
- DAUGHTERS OF THE KING Bible Study Series

Her articles have appeared in numerous magazines, such as *Today's Christian Woman* and *Marriage Partnership*. She has also appeared on many radio and television programs, including *The 700 Club*.

Married for thirty-four years to Larry, her high school sweetheart, Kathy lives in Indio, California, and is the mother of two grown children.

You can learn more about Kathy's ministry at *www.KathyCollardMiller.com*.